MEET THE AUTHORS

Katherine Greenberg and Barbara Kyte have authored several cookbooks, including **Cooking For 1 or 2**. They are known for their knowledge of nutritious foods, which is reflected in their carefully tested recipes. Both have studied with a number of outstanding San Francisco Bay Area cooking teachers.

Due to their busy lifestyles, Katherine and Barbara have become experts in developing great recipes which can be prepared quickly and easily without sacrificing good nutrition.

A handy guide to help you bake faster and better than Grandma!

- **Muffins, Nut Breads and More** is an outstanding collection of quick bread recipes geared for today's busy lifestyles.

- Emphasis is on nutritious ingredients baked into treats the whole family will enjoy.

- Basic recipes offer many variations.

- Time-saving Quick Mix recipes are featured using your own homemade baking mix, which is more nutritious and economical than commercially made ones. See pages 18 and 19.

- Tips on preparation, measurements, ingredients, equivalents and substitutions are found throughout the book.

We dedicate this book to our husbands,
Al and Chuck, and to our little muffins,
John, Tami, David and Tom.
We extend a special thank you to Jackie Walsh.

·MUFFINS·

Nut Breads and More

by
Barbara Kanerva Kyte
Katherine Hayes Greenberg

A Nitty Gritty ® Cookbook

Printed in the United States of America.

ISBN 0-911954-83-X

Editor: Jackie Walsh
Art Director: Mike Nelson
Illustrator: Craig Torlucci

Table of Contents

Introduction

Remember the visits to Grandma's house and the tempting aromas drifting from her kitchen as she baked those mouth-watering breads? Are her delicious goodies more than just memories of the past? Can you fit bread making into your busy life? Yes! Today you can recapture the joy of baking your own bread with a wide variety of quick bread recipes. Made without yeast, quick breads are fast, nutritious and easy to prepare — and they taste just as yummy as the ones Grandma used to make!

Imagine starting your day with a basket of hot, tender biscuits served with a crock of butter and your favorite jam. For dinner, tempt your family with a generous square of corn bread topped with hot and hearty chili. Then satisfy your craving for a sweet treat by nibbling on honey nutbread. You'll find recipes for these and more. So why wait? Prepare your baking pans, preheat your oven and begin!

Prepare Your Pantry with Wholesome Ingredients

FLOUR, the major ingredient in quick breads, contains gluten, which gives the bread its structure. Wheat flours, such as whole wheat and unbleached all purpose flour, may be used separately or together to vary the texture of the bread. Whole wheat flour contains all of the wheat, including the bran and germ. It may be coarse or fine and should be stored in the refrigerator to protect the germ from turning rancid. Non-wheat flours, such as corn, oat, rye and soy, add variety to the taste and texture of quick breads and may be combined with wheat flours.

LIQUIDS, such as milk, fruit juice and water, dissolve the dry ingredients and hold the bread together.

LEAVENING AGENTS, such as baking powder, baking soda, eggs and steam, make the bread rise.

SHORTENINGS, such as butter, margarine and oils, add flavor and tenderness to the bread.

SWEETENERS, such as honey, sugar, molasses and maple syrup, add flavor and moisture to the bread. They also aid in browning. Breads made with liquid sweeteners are more moist and stay fresh longer.

EGGS give your bread rich flavor, texture and protein.

FLAVORINGS determine the character of the bread. By varying the flavorings, you can produce a whole variety of taste sensations from the same basic recipe. Flavorings include salt, extracts, herbs, spices, nuts, seeds, fruits and vegetables.

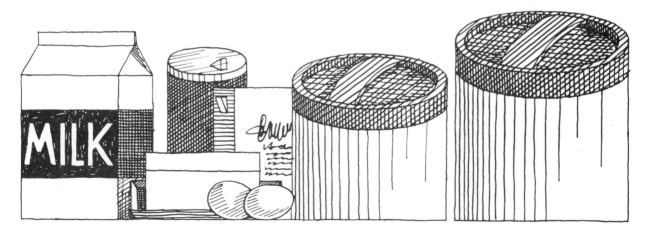

For Good Measure and Perfect Results

Measuring ingredients accurately is an important step in making perfect quick breads. When measuring dry ingredients you do not need to sift. Sifting removes the bran and wheat germ particles from the whole wheat flour. Just spoon the flour, baking soda and baking powder into the measuring cup or spoon and level it off with the flat edge of a knife. When measuring liquids, pour them into a glass measuring cup and hold it at eye level to check for accuracy.

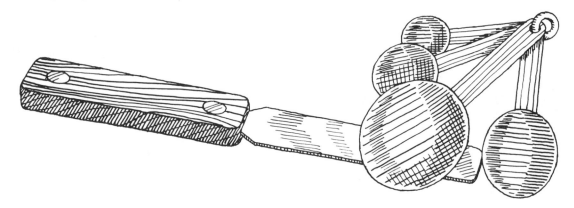

The following list of equivalents will help you with your shopping and measuring.

Apples, 1 lb.	equals	3 medium or 3 cups sliced or grated
Apricots, dried, 1 lb.	equals	3 cups dried or 5 cups cooked
Bananas, 1 lb.	equals	3 whole or 2-1/2 cups sliced, 1-1/2 cups mashed
Cheese, 1 lb.	equals	5 cups grated
Coconut, 1 lb.	equals	5 cups shredded
Dates, unpitted, 1 lb.	equals	2-1/2 cups unpitted or 1-3/4 cups pitted
Lemon, 1 medium	equals	1 tbs. grated rind and 3 tbs. juice
Orange, 1 medium	equals	2 tbs. grated rind and 1/3 cup juice
Prunes, 1 lb.	equals	4-1/2 cups pitted and cooked
Raisins, 1 lb.	equals	3 cups

Natural Substitutions for Better Nutrition

Quick breads made with natural ingredients are tastier and more nutritious. For more fiber and flavor we prefer to use equal parts whole wheat flour and unbleached flour in our recipes instead of using all unbleached flour. Likewise, we prefer honey to sugar. If you do too, be sure to compensate for this by decreasing the quantity of liquid in the recipe (see "Switching Your Sweeteners," page 15).

If you have a favorite quick bread recipe that calls for white flour and sugar, and you want to substitute more nutritious ingredients, use the following guidelines:

FORTIFY YOUR FLOUR

Boost the nutrition of every cup of flour by measuring one tablespoon each instant nonfat dry milk, wheat germ and soy flour into a one-cup measure. Fill the cup with flour and level off with the edge of a knife.

One cup of white flour is equivalent to one cup of whole wheat flour. We like the ratio of half whole wheat and half all-purpose flour. We have found that the texture this ratio produces is most pleasing to everyone. The more whole wheat flour you use, the heavier the texture will be.

SWITCHING YOUR SWEETENERS

One cup of sugar equals 3/4 cup of honey. To substitute honey for sugar, decrease the liquid in the recipe by 1/4 cup. If no liquid is specified, add four tablespoons of flour.

One cup of molasses equals one cup of sugar. To substitute molasses for sugar, decrease the liquid in the recipe by 1/3 cup. Again, if no liquid is specified, add four tablespoons of flour.

Quick Tips for Better Quick Breads

• Avoid the last minute rush at mealtime by mixing the dry ingredients several hours ahead of time, or the night before. It only takes a few minutes to add the liquid ingredients, bake and serve. If you are really on a tight schedule, you might find it convenient to keep a batch of Quick Mix on hand (see pages 18 and 19).

• Unless otherwise specified, have all the ingredients in the recipe at room temperature. This will insure light and tender baked goods.

• Honey will slide right out of the measuring cup if you measure the oil in the recipe first. If no oil is called for in the recipe, coat the measuring cup lightly with oil before measuring the honey.

• Because you may not always have fresh buttermilk on hand, it is convenient to store a box of powdered buttermilk in your cupboard.

• Most quick breads are best when they are served right out of the oven. So, when they are finished baking, serve just enough to go around, and return the rest to the oven to keep warm.

• If you are not going to eat your quick breads within a few days, wrap them tightly in foil and freeze them. They may be frozen up to three months. When you are ready to serve your quick breads, thaw them and warm them in a 350°F. oven.

It takes about five minutes to heat muffins and biscuits, and about ten minutes to heat loaves and coffee cakes.

• Day old muffins and biscuits are delicious when split, toasted and spread with butter.

• For quick and easy clean-up, use any of the following: Teflon baking pans, paper liners for muffins, or disposable foil loaf pans.

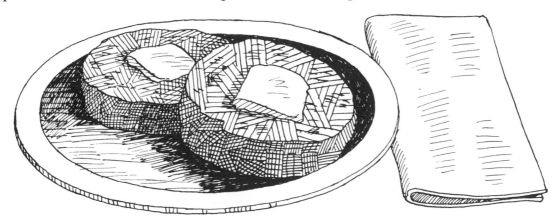

Quick Mixes for Quicker Quick Breads

Don't be without it! Keep our Quick Mix for muffins, breads, biscuits, coffee cakes, pancakes and waffles on hand, ready to use at a moment's notice. Store, tightly covered, for up to two months in the refrigerator and up to four months in the freezer.

All-Purpose Quick Mix
3 cups whole wheat flour
3 cups unbleached all-purpose flour
3 tbs. baking powder
1-1/2 tsp. salt
1 cup butter **or** margarine

Blend flour, baking powder and salt in mixing bowl. Using electric mixer, food processor or pastry blender, cut shortening into flour mixture until it resembles coarse cornmeal. Store tightly covered in the refrigerator or in the freezer. Makes about 8 cups.

Buttermilk Quick Mix

For extra flavor and nutrition, add powdered buttermilk and baking soda to the dry ingredients in the basic Quick Mix recipe.

All-Purpose Quick Mix, page 18
1/2 cup powdered buttermilk
1/2 tsp. baking soda

When you see this symbol: you'll be able to tell at a glance that the recipe beside it is especially easy because it uses Quick Mix.

Muffins, Muffins, Marvelous Muffins

Piping hot muffins are a special treat with meals or as snacks. Made with whole wheat flour, honey and other healthful ingredients, muffins are as nutritious as they are quick to prepare. Once you serve them to your family, they may become a tradition at your house.

The perfect muffin is moist, light and tender. Its texture is even and without tunnels. The top of the muffin is nicely rounded and golden brown. You may ask yourself, "How can I make these perfect muffins?" We have included a list of "secrets" we have accumulated over the years. They work for us, and we are sure that if you follow them, they will work for you!

● Most important of all: in the last step of the recipe, when you are instructed to combine the liquid and dry ingredients, **do not overmix!** Stir the two together only until the dry ingredients become moistened. Overmixing will cause tough muffins with tunnels.

● Because the final step is not a mixing process, but rather a combining process, it is important to have thoroughly stirred together the dry ingredients, and thoroughly beaten together the liquid ingredients, **before** the two are combined.

- When the dry ingredients have been well combined, form a "well" in the center of them. This will facilitate the "combining" process.
- After "combining" the liquid and dry ingredients, let the batter "rest" for a minute or two. This will give the leavening agents a chance to activate.
- Spoon the batter into greased or paper-lined muffin pans, filling them two-thirds full. For a special shape, try mini muffin pans, or bundt muffin pans. Remember, you must adjust the baking time according to the size and shape of the pans you use.
- Bake the muffins in a preheated oven. Test for doneness by gently pressing the center of a muffin. If it springs back, leaving little or no fingerprint, it is done. Or, you may insert a toothpick into a muffin, and if it comes out clean, the muffins are done.
- When you are keeping the muffins warm in the oven, tip each muffin on its side until you are ready for them. This will keep them moist.

QUICK MIX MUFFINS

So quick and easy to make you can serve them often. Be sure to try some of our scrumptious variations on page 25.

1/2 cup milk
1 egg
2 cups Quick Mix (All-Purpose **or** Buttermilk, pages 18 and 19)
1/4 cup sugar

Preheat oven to 400°F. Mix milk and egg together well. Add to Quick Mix and sugar. Stir until just moistened. Fill greased or paper lined muffin pans 2/3 full. Bake for 20 minutes, or until brown. Makes 10 muffins.

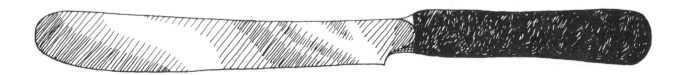

PERFECT MUFFINS

Be creative with these nutritious muffins. There are a lot of choices on page 25.

3/4 cup whole wheat flour
1 cup unbleached all-purpose flour } **or** 1-3/4 cups all-purpose flour
2-1/2 tsp. baking powder
1/2 tsp. salt
1/2 cup milk when using honey (3/4 cup milk when using sugar)
1 egg
1/3 cup oil
1/4 cup honey **or** sugar

Preheat oven to 400°F. Stir together flour, baking powder and salt. Mix milk, egg, oil and honey **or** sugar together well. Add this mixture to dry ingredients. Stir until just moistened. Fill greased or paper-lined muffin pans 2/3 full. Bake for 20 minutes, or until golden brown. Makes 12 muffins.

MUFFIN VARIATIONS

For variety, add one of the following to the dry ingredients called for in our Quick Mix or Perfect Muffins recipe on pages 23 and 24.

- 3 tbs. crisp bacon, crumbled
- 3 tbs. green onion, thinly sliced
- 1/4 tsp. dill, 1/2 tsp. oregano and 1 tbs. snipped parsley
- 1/2 cup shredded cheddar cheese
- 1/2 cup shredded Swiss cheese and 1 tsp. caraway seeds
- 1/4 cup powdered buttermilk and 1/2 tsp. baking soda
- 1/2 cup grated carrot
- 1/2 cup sunflower seeds

Also, if desired:
- Replace the milk with buttermilk and add 1/2 teaspoon baking soda.
- Before baking, sprinkle the top of each muffin with about 1/4 teaspoon paprika, Parmesan cheese **or** sesame seeds.

OATMEAL MUFFINS

Serve these muffins hot with sweet butter and jam . . . . so good!

1 cup whole wheat flour **or** unbleached all-purpose flour
1 cup quick-cooking oats
2-1/2 tsp. baking powder
1/2 tsp. baking soda
1/2 tsp. salt
1/4 cup brown sugar, firmly packed
1 egg
3/4 cup buttermilk
1/3 cup oil

Preheat oven to 400°F. Stir together flour, oats, baking powder, baking soda, salt and brown sugar. Mix egg, buttermilk and oil together well. Add this mixture to dry ingredients. Stir until just moistened. Fill greased or paper-lined muffin pans 2/3 full. Bake for 20 minutes, or until golden brown. Makes 12 muffins.

GRANOLA MUFFINS

Use your favorite granola mix for this lunch box treat.

2 cups Quick Mix (All-Purpose **or** Buttermilk, pages 18 and 19)
1 cup granola
1 egg
1 cup milk
2 tsp. cinnamon **or** nutmeg (optional)

Preheat oven to 400°F. Stir together Quick Mix and granola. Mix egg and milk together well. Add this mixture to dry ingredients. Stir until just moistened. Fill greased or paper-lined muffin pans 2/3 full. If desired, sprinkle batter lightly with cinnamon or nutmeg. Bake for 20 minutes, or until golden brown. Makes 12 muffins.

OLD-FASHIONED BRAN MUFFINS

These delicious muffins taste just like the ones Grandma used to make!

1 cup whole wheat flour **or** all-purpose flour
1 cup unprocessed bran
2-1/2 tsp. baking powder
1/2 tsp. baking soda
1/2 tsp. salt
1/2 cup raisins

1/4 cup sugar **or** honey
1 egg
2/3 cup buttermilk
1/4 cup oil
1/4 cup molasses

Preheat oven to 400°F. Stir together flour, bran, baking powder, baking soda, salt, raisins and sugar. Mix egg, buttermilk, oil and molasses together well. Add this mixture to dry ingredients. Stir until just moistened. Fill greased or paper-lined muffin pans 2/3 full. Bake for 20 minutes, or until done. Makes 12 muffins.

MAKE-AHEAD BRAN MUFFINS

The batter for these wholesome muffins will keep four weeks in the refrigerator.

2 cups all-bran cereal
1 cup crushed shredded wheat cereal
3/4 cup boiling water when using honey (1 cup boiling water when using sugar)
1-1/4 cups whole wheat flour
1-1/4 cups unbleached all-purpose flour
2-1/2 tsp. baking soda
1 tsp. salt
1 cup raisins **or** chopped mixed dried fruit
2 eggs
1/2 cup oil
1/3 cup molasses
3/4 cup honey **or** 1 cup sugar
1 cup buttermilk

Preheat oven to 400°F. Pour boiling water over cereals and set aside. Combine dry ingredients. Mix all liquid ingredients, except buttermilk. Add to dry ingredients. Stir just until moistened. Alternately add cereal mixture and buttermilk. When ready to bake, fill greased or paper-lined muffin pans 2/3 full. Bake for 20 minutes or until done. Makes 30 muffins.

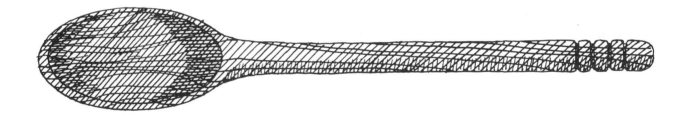

CORN MUFFINS

Serving piping hot with butter.

1/2 cup whole wheat flour
1/2 cup unbleached all-purpose flour } **or** 1 cup all-purpose flour
1 cup yellow cornmeal
1 tbs. baking powder
3/4 tsp. salt
1/4 cup sugar **or** honey
1 cup milk
1 egg
1/4 cup oil

Preheat oven to 400°F. Stir together flour, cornmeal, baking powder, salt and sugar. Mix milk, egg, and oil together well. Add this mixture to dry ingredients. Stir until just moistened. Let batter rest for five minutes. Fill greased or paper-lined muffin pans 2/3 full. Bake for 15 to 20 minutes, or until done. Makes 10 to 12 muffins.

CORN MUFFIN VARIATIONS

Ten different muffins from one basic recipe!

Add one of the following to the dry ingredients:
- 1/4 cup crisp bacon, crumbled
- 1/4 cup green onions, thinly sliced
- 3/4 tsp. dill
- 1/3 cup chopped tomato and 1 tsp. basil
- 1/2 cup grated cheese
- 3 tbs. chopped green chiles

- Fill muffin cups 1/2 full with batter. Drop 1/2 teaspoon jam on each, then fill 2/3 full with batter covering the jam.
- Before baking , sprinkle the top of each muffin with about 1/4 teaspoon Parmesan cheese, sesame seeds **or** a dash of paprika.

SESAME WHEAT GERM MUFFINS

Try this super nutritious muffin!

1 cup whole wheat flour
3/4 cup wheat germ
2-1/2 tsp. baking powder
1/2 tsp. salt
1/4 cup sesame seeds
1 egg
1/2 cup milk
1/4 cup oil
1/4 cup honey

Preheat oven to 400°F. Stir together flour, wheat germ, baking powder, salt and sesame seeds. Mix egg, milk, oil and honey together well. Add this mixture to dry ingredients. Stir until just moistened. Fill greased or paper-lined muffin pans 2/3 full. Bake for 18 minutes, or until golden brown. Makes 10 muffins.

PARMESAN ALMOND MUFFINS

2 cups Quick Mix (All-Purpose **or** Buttermilk, see pages 18 and 19)
1/2 cup grated Parmesan cheese
1/4 cup sugar
1 egg
3/4 cup milk

ALMOND TOPPING:

2 tbs. butter **or** margarine
1 tsp. Worcestershire sauce
1/4 tsp. garlic salt
1/3 cup sliced almonds

Preheat oven to 400°F. Stir together Quick Mix, Parmesan cheese and sugar. Mix egg and milk together well. Add this mixture to dry ingredients. Stir until just moistened. Fill greased or paper-lined muffin pans 2/3 full. Prepare topping by melting butter in saucepan. Stir in remaining topping ingredients. Sprinkle topping over batter, pressing almonds into the batter slightly. Bake for 18 minutes, or until golden brown. Makes 12 muffins.

ZUCCHINI CHEESE MUFFINS

These flavorful muffins will enhance a bowl of hearty soup, a crispy salad or any simple meal. Bake them in mini muffin pans and serve as hors d'oeuvres, too!

2 cups all-purpose flour
1 tbs. baking powder
1/2 tsp. salt
2 tbs. sugar
2 tbs. minced onion
3 slices bacon, fried and crumbled

1/2 cup grated sharp Cheddar cheese
3/4 cup shredded zucchini
1 egg
3/4 cup milk
1/4 cup oil

Preheat oven to 400°F. Stir together flour, baking powder, salt, sugar, onion, bacon, cheese and zucchini. Mix egg, milk and oil together well. Add this mixture to dry ingredients. Stir until just moistened. Fill greased or paper-lined muffin pans 2/3 full. Bake for 20 minutes, or until golden brown. Makes 12 muffins.

QUICK SWEET MUFFINS

This version of our Quick Mix provides a basic sweet muffin. See page 40 for several delicious variations.

2 cups Quick Mix (All-Purpose **or** Buttermilk, see pages 18 and 19)
1/2 cup sugar **or** honey
1/2 cup milk when using honey (2/3 cup milk when using sugar)
1 egg

Preheat oven to 400°F. Mix sugar **or** honey, milk and egg together well. Add this mixture to Quick Mix. Stir until just moistened. Fill greased or paper-lined muffin pans 2/3 full. Bake for 20 minutes, or until golden brown. Makes 10 muffins.

WHOLESOME SWEET MUFFINS

This delicate muffin is ideal for many variations. Children love the surprise of jam baked inside (see page 40).

3/4 cup whole wheat flour
1 cup unbleached all-purpose flour } **or** 1-3/4 cups all-purpose flour
2-1/2 tsp. baking powder
1/2 tsp. salt
1/2 cup milk when using honey (3/4 cup milk when using sugar)
1 egg
1/3 cup oil
1/2 cup honey **or** sugar

Preheat oven to 400°F. Stir together flour, baking powder and salt. Mix milk, egg, oil and honey **or** sugar together well. Add this mixture to dry ingredients. Stir until just moistened. Let sit for one minutes. Fill greased or paper-lined muffin pans 2/3 full. Bake for 20 minutes, or until golden brown. Makes 12 muffins.

SWEET MUFFIN VARIATIONS

Add one of the following to the dry ingredients in the basic recipe:

1/2 cup chopped walnuts
1/2 cup raisins
1/2 cup grated peeled apple
1 cup blueberries (rinsed and drained if they are canned or frozen)
1 tbs. grated orange or lemon rind

Jam Muffins — Place a teaspoon of jam on top of each muffin before baking. Or, fill muffin cups 1/2 full with batter and drop a teaspoon of jam or a slice of banana on each, then fill to 2/3 full with batter.

Streusel Muffins —

3 tbs. flour (whole wheat or all-purpose)
1/4 cup brown sugar, firmly packed
1/2 tsp. cinnamon
1/4 tsp. nutmeg
1/4 cup chopped pecans or walnuts
2 tbs. butter **or** margarine

Combine dry ingredients and nuts. Cut butter in until mixture is crumbly. Sprinkle mixture on muffin batter before baking.

APPLE RAISIN MUFFINS

For all you apple lovers, this muffin has a tempting, spicy apple flavor.

2 cups Quick Mix (All-Purpose **or** Buttermilk, see pages 18 and 19)
1/2 tsp. cinnamon
1/2 cup raisins
1/2 cup brown sugar, firmly packed
1/2 cup peeled and cored apple, grated
1 egg
1/2 cup milk

Preheat oven to 400°F. Combine Quick Mix, cinnamon, raisins, brown sugar and grated apple. Mix egg and milk together well. Add this mixture to dry ingredients. Stir until just moistened. Fill greased or paper-lined muffin pans 2/3 full. Bake for 20 minutes, or until golden brown. Makes 12 muffins.

BLUEBERRY GINGER MUFFINS

Try this delicious and unusual combination.

2-1/2 cups all-purpose flour
1 tbs. baking powder
1/2 tsp. baking soda
1/2 tsp. salt
1/3 cup sugar
1 tsp. cinnamon
1/2 tsp. ginger

1 egg
1 cup buttermilk
1/4 cup oil
1/2 cup dark molasses
1 cup blueberries (rinsed and drained
   if they are canned or frozen)

Preheat oven to 400°F. Stir together flour, baking powder, baking soda, salt, sugar, cinnamon and ginger. Mix milk, buttermilk, oil and molasses together well. Add this mixture to dry ingredients. Stir until just moistened. Gently fold in blueberries. Fill greased or paper-lined muffin pans 2/3 full. Bake for 20 minutes, or until done. Makes 18 muffins.

BANANA OATMEAL MUFFINS

Wake up your family with the mouth-watering aroma of these healthful breakfast muffins. Children are particularly fond of them.

1-1/2 cups all-purpose flour
1 cup quick-cooking oats
2 tsp. baking powder
1 tsp. baking soda
1/2 tsp. salt
1 egg

1/2 cup milk when using honey
    (3/4 cup milk when using sugar)
1/3 cup oil
1/2 cup honey **or** sugar
2/3 cup mashed banana

Preheat oven to 400°F. Stir together flour, oats, baking powder, baking soda and salt. Mix egg, milk, oil, honey **or** sugar and mashed banana together well. Add this mixture to dry ingredients. Stir until just moistened. Fill greased or paper-lined muffin pans 2/3 full. Bake for 20 minutes, or until golden brown. Makes about 16 muffins.

COCONUT PINEAPPLE MUFFINS

These muffins are as light as a tropical breeze.

2 cups all-purpose flour
1 tbs. baking powder
1/2 tsp. salt
1/2 cup **each** sugar and
 flaked coconut
1 egg

1/4 cup oil
1/3 cup milk
1 tsp. vanilla
1 can (8 oz.) crushed pineapple,
 undrained
1 small package sliced almonds
 (optional)

Preheat oven to 400°F. Stir together flour, oats, baking powder, salt, sugar and coconut. Mix egg, oil, milk, vanilla and pineapple together well. Add this mixture to dry ingredients. Stir until just moistened. Fill greased or paper-lined muffin pans 2/3 full. If desired, sprinkle sliced almonds over batter and press them in lightly. Bake for 20 minutes, or until golden brown. Makes 14 muffins.

ORANGE DATE MUFFINS

What a treat with afternoon tea!

1 cup whole wheat flour
1 cup unbleached all-purpose flour } **or** 2 cups all-purpose flour
2-1/2 tsp. baking powder
1/2 tsp. salt
1 tbs. grated orange rind
2/3 cup chopped dates
1 egg
3/4 cup orange juice
1/3 cup oil
1/4 cup honey **or** sugar

Preheat oven to 400°F. Stir together dry ingredients. Mix liquid ingredients together well. Add to dry ingredients. Stir just until moistened. Fill greased or paper-lined muffin pans 2/3 full. Bake for 20 minutes, or until golden brown. Makes 12 muffins.

CRANBERRY ORANGE MUFFINS

These tangy muffins add instant glamour to a roast pork or chicken dinner.

2 cups Quick Mix (All-Purpose **or** Buttermilk, see pages 18 and 19)
1/2 cup sugar
1 tbs. grated orange rind
1/2 cup chopped pecans **or** walnuts
1 egg
1/4 cup orange juice
1 can (8 oz.) whole cranberry sauce

Preheat oven to 400°F. Stir together Quick Mix, sugar, grated orange rind and chopped nuts. Mix egg, orange juice and cranberry sauce together well. Add this mixture to dry ingredients. Stir until just moistened. Fill greased or paper-lined muffin pans 2/3 full. Bake for 25 minutes, or until golden brown. Makes 12 muffins.

MOLASSES PRUNE MUFFINS

Molasses enhances the flavor of the prunes in this nutritious muffin.

2 cups Quick Mix (see page 18)
1/2 cup nuts, chopped
1/2 cup dried prunes, chopped
1 egg
1/2 cup milk
1/2 cup dark molasses

Preheat oven to 400°F. Combine dry ingredients. Mix liquid ingredients together well. Add to dry ingredients. Stir just until moistened. Fill greased or paper-lined muffin pans 2/3 full. Bake for 20 minutes, or until golden brown. Makes 12 muffins.

PERSIMMON MUFFINS

1 cup whole wheat flour
1 cup unbleached all-purpose flour } **or** 2 cups all-purpose flour
1 tbs. baking powder
1/2 tsp. **each** salt, cinnamon and nutmeg
1/4 tsp. cloves
1/2 cup raisins **or** chopped dates
1 egg
1/2 cup milk
1/3 cup oil
1/2 cup honey
1/2 cup mashed persimmon pulp

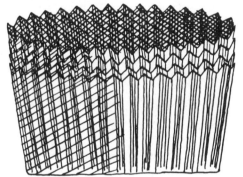

Preheat oven to 400°F. Stir together dry ingredients. Mix liquid ingredients together well. Add to dry ingredients. Stir just until moistened. Fill greased or paper-lined muffin pans 2/3 full. Bake for 20 minutes, or until golden brown. Serve warm with Hard Sauce (see page 180). Makes 14 muffins.

MAPLE NUT MUFFINS

For a change make mini-muffins. Children love them and it makes 42!

1 cup whole wheat flour
1 cup unbleached all-purpose flour } **or** 2 cups all-purpose flour
2-1/2 tsp. baking powder
1/4 tsp. baking soda
1/2 tsp. salt
1/2 cup **each** sugar and chopped nuts
1 egg
1/2 cup milk
1/4 cup **each** maple syrup and oil
1/2 cup sour cream

Preheat oven to 400°F. Stir together flour, baking powder, baking soda, salt, sugar and nuts. Mix egg, milk, syrup, oil and sour cream together well. Add to dry ingredients. Stir until just moistened. Fill greased or paper-lined muffin pans 2/3 full. Bake 20 minutes (15 for mini-muffins). Makes 12 muffins.

LEMON YOGURT MUFFINS

Lemon yogurt is our choice for this moist muffin. Be inventive and substitute your favorite yogurt flavor.

2 cups all-purpose flour
2-1/2 tsp. baking powder
1/2 tsp. **each** baking soda and salt
1 tbs. grated lemon peel
1 egg
1/4 cup oil
1/3 cup honey
1 carton (8 oz.) lemon yogurt

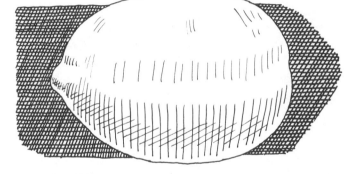

Preheat oven to 400°F. Stir together flour, baking powder, baking soda, salt and grated lemon peel. Mix egg, oil, honey and yogurt together well. Add this mixture to dry ingredients. Stir until just moistened. Fill greased or paper-lined muffin pans 2/3 full. Bake for 18 minutes, or until golden brown. Makes 12 muffins.

Flavorful Sandwich Loaves, Savory Dinner Breads, and Delicious Nut Breads

Delight your family and friends with the moist, flavorful goodness of homemade quick breads by the loaf. If you like the idea of giving something homemade at Christmas time, what better gift than one of our nut breads (see pages 67 through 95). Wrap the bread in bright red or green cellophane and tie it with a bow.

These "helpful hints" should make baking quick breads by the loaf fun and easy for you.

- Like muffins, loaf batter should not be overmixed. When you combine liquid and dry ingredients, try to use as few strokes as possible.
- If the recipe calls for butter or margarine, allow it to soften at room temperature for a few hours before you use it. Then, beat it until it becomes creamy.
- If you always grease and flour your pans, loaves will turn out of them easily.
- Check your bread half-way through its baking time. If the top has become

too brown, cover it with aluminum foil for the rest of baking time.

- The loaf is done if a toothpick inserted into the thickest part comes out clean.
- Cool the bread in its pan for about ten minutes. Then remove from pan and cool completely on a wire rack.
- Your bread will stay fresh longer if you wrap it securely in aluminum foil.

WHOLE WHEAT BREAD

Make delicious sandwiches with this hearty whole wheat bread. It is like brown bread when made with molasses and raisins.

2 cups whole wheat flour
2 tsp. baking powder
1 tsp. baking soda
1/2 tsp. salt
1/2 cup raisins (optional)
1 cup buttermilk
1 egg
1/4 cup oil
2 tbs. molasses, honey **or** sugar

Preheat oven to 350°F. Combine dry ingredients. Mix liquid ingredients together well. Add to dry ingredients. Stir just until blended. Pour batter into a greased and floured loaf pan (9 x 5 x 3 inches). Bake for 45 minutes or until bread tests done. Cool in pan for 5 minutes, then turn out on a wire rack to cool. Makes 1 loaf.

SUPER BREAD

Bring them home for lunch with cream cheese and chopped olives between two slices of Super Bread.

3/4 cup soy flour
1 cup whole wheat flour
1 cup unbleached all-purpose flour } **or** 2 cups all-purpose flour
1/2 cup wheat germ
1/4 cup unprocessed bran
1/3 cup instant nonfat dry milk
1 tbs. baking powder
1 tbs. baking soda
1/2 tsp. salt
1/2 cup **each** chopped dates **or** raisins and chopped nuts
1 cup yogurt
1 egg, well beaten
1/4 cup **each** oil, molasses and honey
1/2 cup orange juice

Preheat oven to 350°F. Stir together soy flour, wheat flour, wheat germ, bran, instant milk, baking powder, baking soda, salt, dates and nuts. Mix yogurt, egg, oil, molasses, honey and orange juice together well. Add this mixture to dry ingredients. Stir until just blended. Spread batter into a greased and floured loaf pan (9 x 5 x 3 inches). Bake for one hour, or until bread tests done. Cover loosely with foil during the last 15 minutes of baking to prevent excess browning. Cool in pan for about 5 minutes, then turn out on a wire rack. Makes 1 loaf.

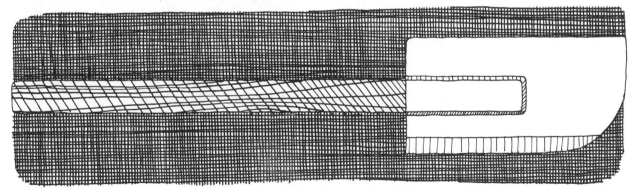

RAISIN OATMEAL BREAD

For a super nutritious sandwich, spread slices of this bread with peanut butter.

2 cups all-purpose flour
1 cup quick cooking oats
1 tbs. baking powder
1/2 tsp. **each** baking soda and salt
1 cup raisins
1-1/4 cups buttermilk
1 egg, well beaten
1/4 cup **each** molasses and oil

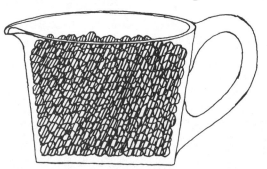

Preheat oven to 350°F. Stir together flour, oats, baking powder, baking soda, salt and raisins. Mix buttermilk, egg, molasses and oil together well. Add this mixture to dry ingredients. Stir until just blended. Pour batter into a greased and floured loaf pan (9 x 5 x 3 inches). Bake for 60 minutes, or until bread tests done. Cool in pan for about 5 minutes, then turn out on a wire rack. Makes 1 loaf.

ZUCCHINI HERB BREAD

1-1/2 cups whole wheat flour
1-1/2 cups unbleached all-purpose flour } **or** 3 cups all-purpose flour
1 tbs. baking powder
1/2 tsp. salt
1 tsp. **each** oregano and basil
1/4 tsp. garlic powder (optional)
1 tbs. minced onion
1/2 cup Parmesan cheese
1 cup grated zucchini
1-1/4 cups milk
1 egg
1/4 cup oil

Preheat oven to 350°F. Stir together dry ingredients. Combine liquid ingredients. Add to dry ingredients. Stir just until blended. Pour batter into a greased and floured loaf pan (9 x 5 x 3 inches). Bake 1 hour and 15 minutes or until done. Makes 1 loaf.

RYE CHEESE BREAD

No need to go out to enjoy a "deli" sandwich. Mound thinly sliced ham or pastrami between two slices of this bread.

1 cup **each** rye flour and unbleached all-purpose flour
1 tbs. baking powder
1/2 tsp. salt
1 tsp. dill
1 tbs. caraway seeds

1 cup **each** shredded
    Swiss cheese and milk
1 egg
1/4 cup oil
2 tbs. honey **or** sugar

Preheat oven to 350°F. Stir together rye flour, all-purpose flour, baking powder, salt, dill, caraway seeds and cheese. Mix milk, egg, oil and honey together well. Add this mixture to dry ingredients. Stir until just blended. Pour batter into a greased and floured loaf pan (9 x 5 x 3 inches). Bake 55 minutes, or until bread tests done. Cool in pan for about 5 minutes, then turn out on a wire rack. Makes 1 loaf.

MEXICAN CORN BREAD

A perfect accompaniment to any South-of-the-Border meal. Try it with our chili on page 185.

1/2 cup whole wheat flour
1/2 cup unbleached all-purpose flour } **or** 1 cup all-purpose flour
3/4 cup yellow cornmeal
1 tbs. baking powder
1/2 tsp. salt
1 tsp. chili powder
2 tbs. minced onion
1/4 cup chopped green chiles (optional)
1 cup drained, Mexican-style whole kernel corn
1 cup shredded Cheddar cheese
1 cup milk
1 egg
2 tbs. **each** oil and honey **or** sugar

Preheat oven to 400°F. Stir together flour, cornmeal, baking powder, salt, chili powder, onion, chiles, corn and cheese. Mix milk, egg, oil and honey together well. Add this mixture to dry ingredients. Stir until just blended. Let rest for 5 minutes. Pour batter into a greased (9 x 9 x 2 inch) baking pan. Bake for 25 minutes, or until golden brown. Makes 8 servings.

PIZZA BREAD

A meal in itself. Pizza bread can double for hors d'oeuvres when cut into small squares.

1 cup whole wheat flour
1 cup unbleached all-purpose flour **or** 2 cups all-purpose flour
1 tbs. baking powder
1/2 tsp. salt
1-1/2 tsp. oregano **PIZZA SAUCE**
3/4 cup milk
1 egg 1 can (6 oz.) tomato paste
1/4 cup oil 1/4 tsp. basil
1 tbs. honey **or** sugar 1/4 tsp. oregano
Topping (see page 65) 1/4 tsp. garlic powder

Preheat oven to 400°F. Stir together flour, baking powder, salt and oregano. Mix milk, egg, oil and honey together well. Add this mixture to dry ingredients. Stir until just blended. Spread batter in a greased baking pan (9 x 9 x 2 inches).

Combine all ingredients for pizza sauce. Spread over batter. Cover with all **or** any combination of topping ingredients as directed. Bake for 30 minutes, or until done. Makes 4 servings.

TOPPING

1/2 cup sliced mushrooms
1/2 cup sliced green peppers
1/4 cup sliced black olives
5 diced anchovies
1/4 cup sliced onions

1/2 cup of any of the following:
    pepperoni, cooked Italian sausage,
    prosciutto, salami, **or** cooked ground beef
    (**or** 1/4 cup of any two).
1 cup shredded Mozzarella cheese

Top pizza sauce with mushrooms, green pepper, olives, anchovies and onions. Sprinkle meat selection over these ingredients. Top with Mozzarella. Bake as directed.

CLASSIC NUT BREAD

This favorite nut bread lends itself to many variations (see page 68).

1 cup whole wheat flour
1 cup unbleached all-purpose flour } **or** 2 cups all-purpose flour
1 tbs. baking powder
1/2 tsp. salt
1 cup chopped pecans **or** walnuts
2/3 cup honey **or** 3/4 cup sugar
3/4 cup milk when using honey (1 cup milk when using sugar)
1 egg
1/4 cup oil

Preheat oven to 350°F. Stir together flour, baking powder, salt and nuts. Mix honey, milk, egg and oil together well. Add this mixture to dry ingredients. Stir until just blended. Pour batter into a greased and floured loaf pan (9 x 5 x 3 inches). Bake for 50 minutes, or until bread tests done. Cool in pan for about 5 minutes, then turn out on a wire rack. Makes 1 loaf.

CLASSIC NUT BREAD VARIATIONS

Try a different one each time you bake Classic Nut Bread on page 67.

- **Apricot Nut Bread**   Add 3/4 cup chopped dried apricots.

- **Date Nut Bread**   Substitute 3/4 cup brown sugar for 3/4 cup sugar and add 1/2 cup chopped dates.

- **Orange Nut Bread**   Substitute orange juice for milk and add 2 tablespoons grated orange peel.

- **Lemon Nut Bread**   Add 1 tablespoon grated lemon peel.

- **Spice Nut Bread**   Add 1/4 teaspoon ground cloves, plus 1/2 teaspoon **each** cinnamon and nutmeg.

- **Pecan, Almond and Walnut Bread**   Replace 1 cup chopped nuts with 1/3 cup **each** chopped pecans, almonds and walnuts.

ORANGE BRAN BREAD

2/3 cup honey
1 cup orange juice
1-1/2 cup all-bran cereal
1 egg
1/4 cup oil
1 cup whole wheat flour
1 cup unbleached all-purpose flour } **or** 2 cups all-purpose flour
1 tbs. baking powder
1/2 tsp. salt
1 tsp. cinnamon
1/4 tsp. cloves
1 tbs. grated orange rind
1 cup golden raisins

Preheat oven to 350°F. Mix honey, orange juice and bran cereal. Combine dry ingredients in a large bowl. Mix egg and oil with bran mixture. Stir into dry ingredients. Pour batter into greased and floured loaf pan (9 x 5 x 3 inches). Bake for 60 minutes or until done. Makes 1 loaf.

BRAN APPLESAUCE LOAF

If you need a mid-morning "pick me up," try a slice of this nutritious bread.

1/2 cup all-bran cereal
1 cup applesauce
1/2 cup butter **or** margarine, softened
3/4 cup honey
1 egg
2 cups all-purpose flour

2 tsp. baking powder
1 tsp. baking soda
1/2 tsp. salt
1 tsp. cinnamon
1/4 tsp. cloves
1/2 cup raisins

Preheat oven to 350°F. Combine all-bran cereal and applesauce. Set aside. Cream butter and honey. Add egg and mix well. Stir together flour, baking powder, baking soda, salt, cinnamon and cloves. Add dry mixture to creamed mixture alternately with applesauce and bran cereal. Mix until just blended. Stir in raisins. Pour batter into a greased and floured loaf pan (9 x 5 x 3 inches). Bake for 60 minutes, or until bread tests done. Cool in pan for about 5 minutes, then turn out on a wire rack. Makes 1 loaf.

HONEY WALNUT BREAD

1/4 cup butter **or** margarine
1 cup honey
1 egg
1 cup milk
1-1/4 cups whole wheat flour
1-1/4 cups unbleached all-purpose flour } **or** 2-1/2 cups all-purpose flour
1-1/2 tsp. baking soda
1/2 tsp. salt
1 cup walnuts, coarsely chopped

Preheat oven to 350°F. Cream butter, adding honey in a fine stream. Beat in egg and milk. Combine dry ingredients. Add to creamed ingredients, mixing well. Stir in nuts. Pour batter into a greased and floured loaf pan (9 x 5 x 3 inches). Garnish the top with walnut halves if desired. Bake for 1 hour and 10 minutes or until bread tests done. Cool in the pan for about 5 minutes, then turn out on a wire rack to cool. Makes 1 loaf.

MORAGA PEAR AND WALNUT BREAD

Living in the midst of pear and walnut orchards in Moraga, California, we were inspired to create this recipe.

1 cup whole wheat flour
1 cup unbleached all-purpose flour } **or** 2 cups all-purpose flour
1 tbs. baking powder
1/2 tsp. salt
1/2 tsp. cinnamon
1/4 tsp. nutmeg
1/4 tsp. ground cloves
1 cup canned pears, drained and chopped
1 cup coarsely chopped walnuts
1/2 cup milk
1 egg
1/4 cup oil
3/4 cup honey

Preheat oven to 350°F. Stir together flour, baking powder, salt, cinnamon, nutmeg, cloves, pears and walnuts. Mix milk, egg, oil and honey together well. Add this mixture to dry ingredients. Stir until just blended. Pour batter into a greased and floured loaf pan (9 x 5 x 3 inches). Bake for 65 minutes, or until done. Cool in pan for about 5 minutes, then turn out on a wire rack. Makes 1 loaf.

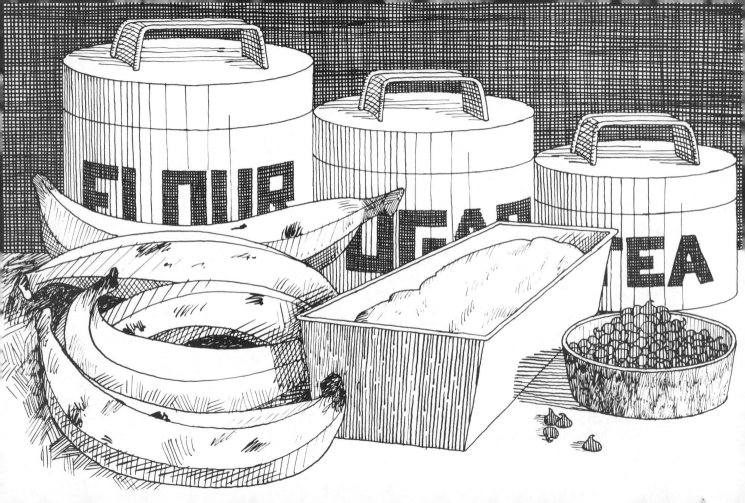

BANANA NUT BREAD

Just about everybody's favorite! What a great way to use ripe bananas. Try it with chocolate chips for a change.

1/3 cup butter **or** margarine, softened
3/4 cup sugar
1 egg
1 cup mashed banana
2 cups all-purpose flour
2-1/2 tsp. baking powder

1/4 tsp. baking soda
1/2 tsp. salt
1 cup chopped pecans **or** walnuts
1/2 cup chocolate chips (optional)
1/2 cup buttermilk

Preheat oven to 350°F. Cream butter and sugar. Mix in egg and banana. Stir together flour, baking powder, baking soda, salt, nuts and chocolate chips. Add this mixture to creamed mixture alternately with buttermilk. Stir until just blended. Pour batter into a greased and floured loaf pan (9 x 5 x 3 inches). Bake for 65 minutes, or until bread tests done. Cool in pan for about 5 minutes, then turn out on a wire rack. Makes 1 loaf.

PEANUT BUTTER BANANA BREAD

Chopped peanuts add extra nutrition to this bread. A slice will boost your energy any time of day.

1/2 cup crunchy peanut butter
1/4 cup oil
1/2 cup honey
1 egg
1 cup mashed banana
2 cups whole wheat flour

1 cup wheat germ
1 tbs. baking powder
1/2 tsp. salt
1/2 cup chopped peanuts (optional)
3/4 cup milk

Preheat oven to 350°F. Mix peanut butter, oil, honey, egg and mashed banana together well. Combine flour, wheat germ, baking powder, salt and peanuts. Add dry ingredients to peanut butter mixture alternately with milk. Spread batter in a greased and floured loaf pan (9 x 5 x 3 inches). Bake for 1 hour, or until bread tests done. Cool in pan for about 5 minutes, then turn out on a wire rack. Makes 1 loaf.

BUTTERSCOTCH POPPY SEED LOAF

1/4 cup butter **or** margarine, softened
1 cup dark brown sugar, firmly packed
1 egg
2 tsp. vanilla
2 cups all-purpose flour
2 tsp. baking powder
1 tsp. baking soda
1/2 tsp. salt
3 tbs. poppy seeds
1 cup buttermilk

Preheat oven to 350°F. Cream butter and sugar. Stir in egg and vanilla. Combine flour, baking powder, baking soda, salt and poppy seeds. Add this mixture to creamed mixture alternately with buttermilk. Stir until just blended. Pour batter into a greased and floured loaf pan (9 x 5 x 3 inches). Bake for 60 minutes, or until bread tests done. Cool in pan for about 5 minutes, then turn out on a wire rack. Makes 1 loaf.

TUTTI-FRUTTI NUT BREAD

A festive bread with a delightful blend of fruit and nuts.

1 cup whole wheat flour
1 cup unbleached all-purpose flour } **or** 2 cups all-purpose flour
1 tbs. baking powder
1/2 tsp. salt
3/4 cup brown sugar, firmly packed
1/2 cup **each** grated apple, chopped dried apricots and dates
1 cup nuts, chopped
3/4 cup milk
1 egg
1/4 cup oil

Preheat oven to 350°F. Stir together dry ingredients. Mix liquid ingredients together well. Add to dry ingredients. Stir just until blended. Pour batter in a greased and floured loaf pan (9 x 5 x 3 inches). Bake for 1 hour, or until bread tests done. If desired, pour brandy over the loaf while still warm. Turn out on a wire rack to cool. Makes 1 loaf.

SHERRIED PUMPKIN LOAF

1 cup whole wheat flour
1 cup unbleached all-purpose flour } **or** 2 cups all-purpose flour
1 tbs. baking powder
1/2 tsp. **each** salt, cinnamon and nutmeg
1/4 tsp. ground cloves
1 cup sugar
1 cup chopped pecans **or** walnuts
1/2 cup cream sherry
2 eggs
1/2 cup oil
1 cup canned pumpkin

Preheat oven to 350°F. Combine dry ingredients. Mix liquid ingredients well. Add to dry ingredients. Stir just until blended. Pour batter into a greased and floured loaf pan (9 x 5 x 3 inches). Bake for 65 minutes or until done.

BOURBON PECAN BREAD

Serve this to your yuletide party guests.

2 cups unbleached all-purpose flour
2-1/2 tsp. baking powder
1/2 tsp. baking soda
1/2 tsp. salt
1-1/2 tsp. mace **or** nutmeg
1 cup chopped pecans **or** walnuts

1 cup sugar
1 cup sour cream
1 egg
1/4 cup oil
1/2 cup bourbon

Preheat oven to 350°F. Stir together flour, baking powder, baking soda, salt, mace, nuts and sugar. Mix sour cream, egg, oil and bourbon together well. Add this mixture to dry ingredients. Stir just until blended. Pour batter into a greased and floured loaf pan (9 x 5 x 3 inches), or into three greased and floured small loaf pans (6 x 3 x 2 inches). If desired, sprinkle batter with sugar before baking. Bake standard loaf for 1 hour, or until bread tests done. Bake three small loaves for 45 minutes, or until done. Cool in pan for about 5 minutes, then turn out on a wire rack. Makes 1 large loaf, or three small loaves.

CHEDDAR BEER BREAD

Beer gives this bread a slightly sourdough flavor.

2-1/2 cups all-purpose flour
1-1/2 tsp. baking soda
1/2 tsp. **each** salt and nutmeg
3/4 cup brown sugar, firmly packed
1 cup **each** raisins, shredded Cheddar cheese and chopped pecans **or** walnuts
1-1/4 cup beer
1 egg
1/4 cup oil

Preheat oven to 350°F. Stir together flour, baking soda, salt, nutmeg, brown sugar, raisins, cheese and nuts. Mix beer, egg and oil together well. Add this mixture to dry ingredients. Stir just until blended. Pour batter into a greased and floured loaf pan (9 x 5 x 3 inches). Bake for 60 minutes, or until bread tests done. Cool in pan for about 5 minutes, then turn out on a wire rack. Makes 1 loaf.

TOASTED COCONUT BREAD

Toasting the coconut enhances this bread's nut-like flavor.

1 cup shredded coconut
2 cups unbleached all-purpose flour
1 tbs. baking powder
1/2 tsp. salt
1 cup milk

1 egg
1/4 cup oil
3/4 cup sugar
1 tsp. vanilla

Preheat oven to 350°F. Place coconut in a large, shallow baking pan in preheated oven. Stir occasionally until it is golden brown (about 5 minutes). Stir together flour, baking powder, salt and toasted coconut. Mix milk, egg, oil and vanilla together well. Add to dry ingredients. Stir until just blended. Pour batter into a greased and floured loaf pan (9 x 5 x 3 inches). Bake for 1 hour, or until done. Cool in pan for about 5 minutes, then turn out on a wire rack. Makes 1 loaf.

SWEET POTATO BREAD

1 cup whole wheat flour
1 cup unbleached all-purpose flour } **or** 2 cups all-purpose flour
1 tbs. baking powder
1/2 tsp. salt
1 cup sugar
1/4 tsp. ginger
1/2 tsp. cinnamon
1/4 tsp. nutmeg
1/2 cup chopped pecans **or** walnuts
1/2 cup orange juice
1 egg
1/3 cup oil
16 oz. sweet potatoes **or** yams, drained and mashed (1-1/3 cups)

Preheat oven to 350°F. Combine flour, baking powder, salt, sugar, ginger, cinnamon, nutmeg and nuts. Mix orange juice, egg, oil and sweet potatoes together well. Add this mixture to dry ingredients. Stir until just blended. Pour batter into a greased and floured loaf pan (9 x 5 x 3 inches). Bake for 1 hour and 15 minutes, or until bread tests done. Cool in pan for about 5 minutes, then turn out on a wire rack. Makes 1 loaf.

28 FAVORITE QUICK MIX NUT BREADS

Find your favorite flavor on our chart and bake a delicious Quick Mix loaf. With Quick Mix on hand (see pages 18 and 19), you can prepare one or more loaves in no time, by simply following these basic directions:

Combine the dry ingredients. Mix the liquid ingredients together well. Add to dry ingredients. Stir until just blended. Pour batter into a greased and floured loaf pan (9 x 5 x 3 inches). Bake in a preheated 350°F. oven, for 55 to 65 minutes, or until bread tests done. Or, bake in three small loaf pans (6 x 3 x 2 inches), for 45 to 50 minutes. Cool in pans for about 5 minutes, then turn out on a wire rack.

Put on your thinking cap and be creative with the basic recipes. Add an unusual spice, like cardamom or anise. Mix and match different nuts, fruits and vegetables. Use either honey or sugar. We have included proportions for both. Take an old family favorite and improvise or create a new one!

	ALMOND	APPLE	APRICOT	BANANA
QUICK MIX	3-1/2 cups	3-1/2 cups	3-1/2 cups	3-1/2 cups
Spices and Flavorings	1 tsp. almond extract	1 tsp. cinnamon		
Nuts	1 cup sliced almonds	1 cup chopped nuts	1 cup chopped nuts	1 cup chopped nuts
Variation		1 cup apple, shredded	1 cup diced, dried apricots	1 cup mashed banana
Egg	1	1	1	1
Honey and Liquid	2/3 cup honey and 1 cup milk	2/3 cup honey and 2/3 cup milk or apple juice	3/4 cup honey and 3/4 cup apricot nectar	2/3 cup honey 1/3 cup milk
OR **Sugar and Liquid**	3/4 cup sugar and 1-1/4 cups milk	3/4 cup brown sugar, firmly packed, and 1 cup milk or apple juice	1 cup sugar and 1 cup apricot nectar	3/4 cup sugar and 1/2 cup milk

	BLUEBERRY	BUTTER-SCOTCH CHIP	CARROT	CHOCOLATE OR CAROB CHIP
QUICK MIX	3-1/2 cups	3-1/2 cups	3-1/2 cups	3-1/2 cups
Spices and Flavorings	1 tsp. grated orange peel	1 tsp. vanilla	1 tsp. cinnamon	
Nuts	1 cup chopped nuts	1 cup chopped nuts	1 cup chopped nuts	1 cup chopped nuts
Variation	1 cup blueberries	1 cup butter-scotch chips	1 cup grated carrot	1 cup chocolate or carob chips
Egg	1	1	1	1
Honey and Liquid	2/3 cup honey and 1 cup orange juice	2/3 cup honey and 1 cup milk	2/3 cup honey and 2/3 cup milk	2/3 cup honey and 1 cup milk
OR **Sugar and Liquid**	3/4 cup sugar and 1 cup orange juice	3/4 cup brown sugar, firmly packed, and 1-1/4 cups milk	3/4 cup brown sugar, firmly packed, and 1 cup milk	3/4 cup sugar and 1-1/4 cups milk

	COCONUT	CRANBERRY	DATE	FIG
QUICK MIX	3-1/2 cups	3-1/2 cups	3-1/2 cups	3-1/2 cups
Spices and Flavorings		1 tbs. grated orange peel	1 tbs. grated orange peel	1/2 tsp. cinnamon and 1/2 tsp. allspice
Nuts	1 cup chopped nuts	1 cup chopped nuts	1 cup chopped nuts	1 cup chopped nuts
Variation	3/4 cup coconut	3/4 cup cranberries, chopped	1 cup dates, chopped	1 cup chopped, dried figs
Egg	1	1	1	1
Honey and Liquid	2/3 cup honey and 1 cup milk	2/3 cup honey and 3/4 cup orange juice	2/3 cup honey and 3/4 cup orange juice	2/3 cup honey and 3/4 cup orange juice
OR **Sugar and Liquid**	3/4 cup brown sugar, firmly packed, and 1-1/4 cups milk	3/4 cup brown sugar, firmly packed, and 1 cup orange juice	3/4 cup sugar and 1 cup orange juice	3/4 cup sugar and 1 cup orange juice

	GRANOLA	LEMON	ORANGE	PEACH
QUICK MIX	3-1/2 cups	3-1/2 cups	3-1/2 cups	3-1/2 cups
Spices and Flavorings		2 tbs. grated lemon peel	2 tbs. grated orange peel	1 tsp. cinnamon
Nuts		1 cup chopped nuts	1 cup chopped nuts	1 cup chopped nuts
Variation	1 cup granola			1 cup diced, dried peaches
Egg	1	1	1	1
Honey and Liquid	2/3 cup honey and 1 cup milk, apple or orange juice	2/3 cup honey and 1 cup milk	2/3 cup honey and 1 cup orange juice	2/3 cup honey and 3/4 cup orange juice
Sugar and Liquid	3/4 cup sugar and 1-1/4 cups milk, apple or orange juice	3/4 cup sugar and 1-1/4 cups milk	3/4 cup sugar and 1-1/4 cups orange juice	3/4 cup sugar and 1 cup orange juice

OR

	PEANUT	PEAR	PECAN	PINEAPPLE
QUICK MIX	3-1/2 cups	3-1/2 cups	3-1/2 cups	3-1/2 cups
Spices and Flavorings		1 tsp. cinnamon		1 tbs. grated orange peel
Nuts	1 cup chopped peanuts	1 cup chopped nuts	1 cup chopped pecans	1 cup chopped nuts
Variation		1 cup diced, dried pears		2/3 cup drained crushed pineapple
Egg	1	1	1	1
Honey and Liquid	2/3 cup honey and 1 cup milk	2/3 cup honey and 3/4 cup orange juice	2/3 cup honey and 1 cup milk	2/3 cup honey and 2/3 cup orange juice
OR **Sugar and Liquid**	3/4 cup brown sugar, firmly packed, and 1-1/4 cups milk	3/4 cup sugar and 1 cup orange juice	3/4 cup brown sugar, firmly packed, and 1-1/4 cups milk	3/4 cup brown sugar, firmly packed, and 3/4 cup orange juice

	PRUNE	PUMPKIN	RAISIN	SPICE
QUICK MIX	3-1/2 cups	3-1/2 cups	3-1/2 cups	3-1/2 cups
Spices and Flavorings	1 tbs. grated orange peel	1 tsp. cinnamon 1/2 tsp. allspice		1/2 tsp. cinnamon 1/2 tsp. nutmeg 1/4 tsp. cloves
Nuts	1 cup chopped nuts	1 cup chopped nuts	1 cup chopped nuts	1 cup chopped nuts
Variation	1 cup chopped, dried prunes	1 cup canned pumpkin	1 cup raisins	
Egg	1	1	1	1
Honey and Liquid	2/3 cup honey and 3/4 cup prune juice	2/3 cup honey and 1/3 cup milk	2/3 cup honey and 3/4 cup milk or orange juice	2/3 cup honey and 1 cup milk
OR **Sugar and Liquid**	3/4 cup sugar and 1 cup prune juice	3/4 cup sugar and 1/2 cup milk	3/4 cup sugar and 1 cup milk or orange juice	3/4 cup sugar and 1-1/4 cups milk

	SWEET POTATO OR YAM	WALNUT	YOGURT	ZUCCHINI
QUICK MIX	3-1/2 cups	3-1/2 cups	3-1/2 cups	3-1/2 cups
Spices and Flavorings	1 tsp. cinnamon 1/2 tsp. allspice		1/2 tsp. baking soda	1 tsp. cinnamon
Nuts	1 cup chopped nuts	1 cup chopped walnuts	1 cup chopped nuts	1 cup chopped nuts
Variation	1 cup mashed, cooked sweet potato		1 cup yogurt, any flavor	1 cup shredded zucchini
Egg	1	1	1	1
Honey and Liquid	2/3 cup honey and 1/3 cup milk	2/3 cup honey and 1 cup milk	2/3 cup honey and 1/2 cup milk	2/3 cup honey and 2/3 cup milk
OR **Sugar and Liquid**	3/4 cup sugar and 1/2 cup milk	3/4 cup sugar and 1-1/4 cups milk	3/4 cup sugar and 2/3 cup milk	3/4 cup brown sugar, firmly packed, and 1 cup milk

Biscuits and Special Biscuit Breads

No pre-packaged baking mix can rival the flavor of homemade, fresh-baked biscuits, or biscuit-type breads such as scones, shortcake and pinwheels.

Here are a few hints that will help you produce delicious biscuits:

- Use chilled butter or margarine.
- Cut the butter or margarine into the dry ingredients, using a pastry blender or two knives, until the mixture resembles coarse cornmeal.
- When adding liquid to the dry ingredients, stir with a fork only until the mixture is moistened.
- To knead the dough, turn the mixture onto a floured surface. Grasp the dough with both hands and gently push it away from you with the heels of your hands. Repeat this procedure ten to twelve times.
- Roll or pat the dough 1/2-inch thick, or 1/4-inch thick and fold over. Cut with a 2-1/2-inch biscuit cutter.
- For biscuits with soft sides, place them close together on a baking sheet. If crisp biscuits are preferred, place them two inches apart on baking sheet.

For a brown crust, brush tops of biscuits with milk before baking.

QUICK MIX BISCUITS

The quickest of the quick. Just mix, bake and serve. Since these are so easy to put together, why not take a few minutes and add any of the variations on page 101.

2-1/2 cups Quick Mix (All-Purpose **or** Buttermilk, pages 18 and 19)
1/2 cup milk

Preheat oven to 450°F. Combine Quick Mix and milk. Knead gently twelve times. Roll or pat dough 1/2-inch thick, or 1/4-inch thick and fold over. Cut into squares, or 2-1/2 inch rounds. Bake on an ungreased baking sheet for 12 minutes, or until golden brown. Makes 10 biscuits.

For Drop Biscuits, decrease Quick Mix to 2 cups and combine with milk. Drop by tablespoonfuls onto a greased baking sheet. Bake for 10 to 12 minutes, or until golden brown. Makes 10 biscuits.

BAKING POWDER BISCUITS

These are the biscuits Grandma used to make.

1 cup whole wheat flour
1 cup unbleached all-purpose flour } **or** 2 cups all-purpose flour
1 tbs. baking powder
1/2 tsp. salt
1/3 cup butter **or** margarine
3/4 cup milk

Preheat oven to 450°F. Stir together flour, baking powder and salt. Cut butter into dry ingredients until the mixture resembles coarse cornmeal. Add milk and stir slightly. Knead gently twelve times. Roll or pat dough 1/2-inch thick or roll 1/4-inch thick and fold over. Cut into squares, 2-1/2 inch rounds, or other interesting shapes with cookie cutters. Bake on an ungreased baking sheet for 12 minutes, or until golden brown. Makes 10 biscuits.

BUTTERMILK BISCUITS

Buttermilk gives biscuits a lighter texture and wonderful flavor.

1 cup whole wheat flour
1 cup unbleached all-purpose flour } **or** 2 cups all-purpose flour
1 tbs. baking powder
1/2 tsp. baking soda
1/2 tsp. salt
1/3 cup butter **or** margarine
3/4 cup buttermilk

Preheat oven to 400°F. Stir together flour, baking powder, baking soda and salt. Cut butter into dry ingredients until the mixture resembles coarse cornmeal. Add buttermilk and stir slightly. Knead gently twelve times. Roll or pat dough 1/2-inch thick or roll 1/4-inch thick and fold over. Cut into squares, 2-1/2 inch rounds, or other interesting shapes with cookie cutters. Bake on an ungreased baking sheet for 12 minutes, or until golden brown. Makes 10 biscuits.

BISCUIT VARIATIONS

Create different biscuits by adding one of the following to the dry ingredients called for in our Quick Mix, Baking Powder or Buttermilk Biscuit recipes.

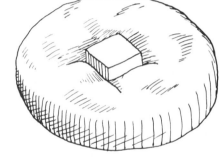

- 3 tbs. crumbled, crisp bacon
- 1/4 cup snipped parsley
- 1/4 cup grated carrot
- 1/4 tsp. thyme, basil **or** marjoram
- 2 tsp. poppy, sesame **or** caraway seeds
- 3 tbs. grated onion
- 1/2 cup grated cheese
- 1/2 cup chopped nuts
- 1/2 cup chopped dates **or** raisins
- **Beverly's Buns** — Dip a sugar cube in orange juice and press into the center of each biscuit.
- **Drop Biscuits** — Increase the milk to 1 cup. Drop the batter by tablespoonfuls onto a greased baking sheet. Add any one of the above variations to the dry ingredients.

continued

Biscuit Variations Continued

- **Filled Biscuits** — Roll the dough 1/4-inch thick. Spread any of the above variations or 1/4 teaspoon of jam on half of the dough; fold the other half over. Cut in squares or triangles.
- **Sour Cream Biscuits** — Substitute 1 cup sour cream for the milk and add 1/2 teaspoon baking soda.
- **Pinwheel Biscuits** — Roll the dough 1/4-inch thick, into a 10 x 16-inch rectangle. Brush with about 1/3 cup melted butter or margarine and spread with any of the variations below. Roll as for jelly roll (starting at the long end). Cut in 1-inch slices and bake. Makes 16 biscuits.
  Variations:
  1 cup grated cheese and 1/4 cup sliced ripe olives **or** sliced green onions
  1/2 cup sugar and 1 tsp. cinnamon, combined
  1/2 cup brown sugar, firmly packed, and 1/2 cup chopped pecans **or** walnuts
  1/2 cup jam or marmalade
  1/2 cup sugar, 1 tbs. grated orange peel and 1/3 cup currants

CORNMEAL BISCUITS

3/4 cup whole wheat flour
3/4 cup unbleached all-purpose flour } **or** 1-1/2 cups all-purpose flour
1/2 cup yellow cornmeal
2 tsp. baking powder
1/2 tsp. baking soda
1/2 tsp. salt
1/3 cup butter **or** margarine
1 cup sour cream
1 tbs. honey **or** sugar

Preheat oven to 450°F. Stir together flour, cornmeal, baking powder, baking soda and salt. Cut butter into the mixture until it resembles coarse cornmeal. Add sour cream and honey. Stir slightly. Knead twelve times. Roll or pat dough 1/2-inch thick, or 1/4-inch thick and fold over. Cut into 2-1/2-inch rounds. If desired, sprinkle with paprika. Bake on an ungreased baking sheet for 10 minutes, or until golden brown. Makes 10 biscuits.

RYE BISCUITS

When you go on your next picnic, use these biscuits instead of "regular" bread for mini sandwiches.

1 cup **each** all-purpose flour and rye flour
1 tbs. baking powder
1/2 tsp. **each** baking soda and salt
1 tbs. caraway seeds
1/3 cup butter **or** margarine
3/4 cup buttermilk

Preheat oven to 425°F. Stir together flours, baking powder, baking soda, salt and caraway seeds. Cut butter into dry ingredients until the mixture resembles coarse cornmeal. Add buttermilk and stir slightly. Knead dough gently twelve times. Roll or pat dough 1/2-inch thick, or 1/4-inch thick and fold over. Cut into squares, or 2-1/2-inch rounds. Bake on an ungreased baking sheet for 12 minutes, or until done. Makes 10 biscuits.

SWEET BISCUITS

These delicate biscuits have a wonderful flavor and texture.

2 cups all-purpose flour
1 tbs. baking powder
1/2 tsp. salt
1/2 cup butter **or** margarine
3/4 cup cream
1 tbs. honey
1/4 cup milk
2 tbs. sugar

Preheat oven to 450°F. Stir together flour, baking powder and salt. Cut butter into dry ingredients until the mixture resembles coarse cornmeal. Add cream and honey. Stir until blended. Knead gently twelve times. Roll or pat dough 1/2-inch thick, or 1/4-inch thick and fold over. Cut into 2-1/2-inch rounds. Brush with milk and sprinkle with sugar. Bake on an ungreased baking sheet for 12 minutes, or until golden brown. Makes 10 biscuits.

SWEET POTATO BISCUITS

3/4 cup whole wheat flour
3/4 cup unbleached all-purpose flour } **or** 1-1/2 cups all-purpose flour
2-1/2 tsp. baking powder
1/2 tsp. salt
1 tbs. brown sugar, firmly packed
1/3 cup butter **or** margarine
1/4 cup milk
1/2 cup cooked **or** canned sweet potato, mashed
1 tsp. cinnamon (optional)

Preheat oven to 425°F. Stir together flour, baking powder, salt and brown sugar. Cut butter into dry ingredients until the mixture resembles coarse cornmeal. Stir in milk and sweet potato. Knead gently twelve times. Roll or pat dough 1/2-inch thick, or 1/4-inch thick and fold over. Cut into 2-1/2-inch rounds. If desired, sprinkle with cinnamon. Bake on an ungreased baking sheet for 10 to 12 minutes, or until done. Makes about 10 biscuits.

ENERGY PACKED DROP BISCUITS

Serve with cold milk for a nutritious snack.

1 cup all-purpose flour
1/2 cup soy flour
1/3 cup wheat germ
2 tbs. unprocessed bran
1/3 cup instant nonfat dry milk
1 tbs. baking powder
1/2 tsp. baking soda
1/4 tsp. salt
1/3 cup butter **or** margarine
1/4 cup **each** chopped dates **or** raisins and chopped nuts **or** sunflower seeds
1/2 cup plain yogurt
2 tbs. **each** molasses and honey
1/4 cup orange juice

Preheat oven to 400°F. Stir together flour, soy flour, wheat germ, bran, powdered milk, baking powder, baking soda and salt. Cut butter into dry ingredients until the mixture resembles coarse cornmeal. Add the chopped dates and nuts. Mix yogurt, molasses, honey and orange juice together well. Add this mixture to dry ingredients. Stir slightly until moistened. Drop by tablespoonfuls onto a greased baking sheet. Bake for 10 minutes, or until golden brown. Makes 16 drop biscuits.

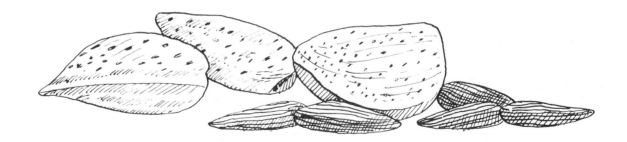

HERB CHEESE DROP BISCUITS

For a light meal, split these biscuits and top with Ratatouille (page 183).

2 cups Quick Mix (All-Purpose **or** Buttermilk, pages 18 and 19)
1/4 tsp. dill
1/4 tsp. oregano
3/4 cup grated cheddar cheese
3/4 cup milk

Preheat oven to 450°F. Stir together Quick Mix, dill, oregano and cheese. Add milk and stir until moistened. Divide into 6 large drop biscuits. Bake on a greased baking sheet for 15 minutes, or until golden brown. Makes 6 large or 12 regular drop biscuits.

SESAME SEED DROP BISCUITS

A blend of natural ingredients creates this wholesome biscuit.

1-1/2 cups whole wheat flour
1/2 cup wheat germ
1 tbs. baking powder
1/2 tsp. baking soda
1/2 tsp. salt
1/3 cup butter **or** margarine

1 egg
1 cup buttermilk
1 tbs. honey **or** sugar
1/4 cup melted butter **or** margarine
1/2 cup sesame seeds

Preheat oven to 400°F. Mix flour, wheat germ, baking powder, baking soda and salt together. Cut in butter until mixture resembles coarse cornmeal. Combine egg, buttermilk and honey. Stir this mixture into dry ingredients. Drop by tablespoonfuls onto a greased baking sheet. Brush with melted butter and sprinkle with sesame seeds. Bake 12 to 15 minutes. Makes 20 biscuits.

BREAD STICKS

Great to serve with a soup and salad meal.

2 cups all-purpose flour
1 tbs. baking powder
1/2 tsp. salt
1/4 cup butter **or** margarine

2 eggs
1/2 cup milk
1/4 cup melted butter **or** margarine
2 tbs. sesame seeds (optional)

Preheat oven to 450°F. Stir together flour, baking powder and salt. Cut un-melted butter into dry ingredients until the mixture resembles coarse cornmeal. Mix together eggs and milk. Stir into dry mixture until moistened. Roll or pat the dough 1/2-inch thick in the shape of a rectangle of about 8 x 6-inches. Cut into sticks, 4 inches long and 1/2-inch wide. Roll gently to round the sides. Sprinkle with flour if the dough is too sticky to handle easily. Brush a cookie sheet with 1 tablespoon of the melted butter. Place bread sticks on the sheet and brush with remaining melted butter. If desired, sprinkle with sesame seeds. Bake for 12 minutes, or until golden brown. Makes 24 bread sticks.

CHEESE CORN STICKS

Instead of corn on the cob, serve Cheese Corn Sticks at your next barbecue.

1 cup all-purpose flour
3/4 cup cornmeal
1 tbs. baking powder
1/2 tsp. **each** baking soda and salt
1/2 cup shredded Cheddar **or** Monterey Jack cheese
1/4 cup honey **or** sugar
1 cup sour cream
1 egg
2 tbs. oil

Preheat oven to 425°F. Stir together flour, cornmeal, baking powder, baking soda, salt and cheese. Mix honey, sour cream, egg and oil together well. Add this mixture to dry ingredients. Stir until just blended. Let batter rest for 5 minutes. Fill each greased section of a corn stick pan 2/3 full. Bake for 12 to 15 minutes, or until golden brown. Makes 18 corn sticks.

SCONES

Scones are a British invention which can be cut into a variety of shapes such as squares, diamonds, hearts or triangles. Serve hot from the oven with butter and jam, and to be completely authentic, tea.

1 cup whole wheat flour
1 cup unbleached all-purpose flour } **or** 2 cups all-purpose flour
1 tbs. baking powder
1/2 tsp. salt
6 tbs. butter **or** margarine
1/2 cup milk
1 egg
2 tbs. honey **or** sugar

Preheat oven to 425°F. Mix together flour, baking powder and salt. Cut butter into dry ingredients until the mixture resembles coarse cornmeal. Combine milk, egg and honey. Stir into dry ingredients until moistened. Knead fifteen times on a floured surface. Divide dough in half and form into two balls. Roll or pat each one

1/2-inch thick, forming 2 six-inch circles. Cut each circle into 6 wedges. Or, you may wish to pat the dough 1/2-inch thick and cut into squares, triangles or diamonds. Bake on an ungreased baking sheet for 12 minutes, or until golden brown.

For variety add 1/2 cup currants, raisins **or** chopped nuts to the dry ingredients. Use buttermilk in place of milk and add 1/2 teaspoon of baking soda.

Grandpa Jack rolls his scones 1/4-inch thick, folds the dough over once, and cuts it into triangles. He brushes the top of the scones with egg white, then sprinkles them with sugar before baking.

SHORTCAKE

There is hardly any better base for fresh fruit than shortcake. Top with any fresh fruit in season and add a dollop of whipped cream for good measure.

1 cup whole wheat flour
1 cup unbleached all-purpose flour } **or** 2 cups all-purpose flour
1 tbs. baking powder
1/2 tsp. salt
1/2 cup butter **or** margarine
2/3 cup light cream
1 egg
2 tbs. honey **or** sugar
1 tbs. sugar

Preheat oven to 450°F. Mix flour, baking powder and salt together. Cut butter into dry ingredients until the mixture resembles coarse cornmeal. Stir cream, egg and honey together well. Add them to the dry mixture. Stir until moistened. Pat dough into a greased and floured 8 x 8 x 2-inch square pan or an 8 x 1-1/2-inch round pan and sprinkle with sugar. Bake for 15 minutes, or until golden brown. Serve warm, split and filled with fruit and whipped cream.

For individual shortcakes prepare shortcake dough. Knead dough gently on a floured surface, then pat or roll 1/2-inch thick. Cut eight shortcakes with a 2-1/2-inch round cutter. Sprinkle with sugar. Bake 8 to 10 minutes on an ungreased baking sheet. Serve as above.

QUICK HOT CROSS BUNS

Hot cross buns are traditionally served at Easter time. Our families often request them for a special birthday breakfast.

2 cups Quick Mix (All-Purpose **or** Buttermilk, pages 18 and 19)
1/4 cup currants **or** raisins
1/4 cup mixed candied fruit
1 tsp. cinnamon
1 tsp. instant coffee powder
1/4 cup sugar
1/2 cup milk
1 egg yolk
1 tbs. water
Frosting (see page 119)

Preheat oven to 450°F. Stir together Quick Mix, currants, candied fruit, cinnamon, coffee powder and sugar. Add milk and stir to form a soft dough. Knead on a floured surface 25 times. Shape into 8 balls and place close together in a greased and floured 8-inch round baking pan. Combine egg yolk and water. Brush over tops of buns. Bake for 15 minutes, or until golden brown. Cool and decorate with frosting as directed.

FROSTING

1/3 cup powdered sugar
1 tsp. milk

Combine ingredients. Decorate each bun with an "X." Makes 8 buns.

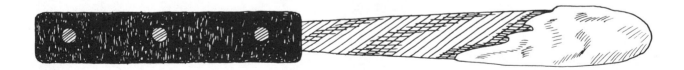

RAISIN NUT PINWHEELS

Our children love these for breakfast. They are so much better than the refrigerated variety sold in supermarkets.

2 cups Quick Mix (See pages 18 and 19)
1/4 tsp. baking soda
1/2 cup raisins
1/2 cup sour cream
1/4 cup milk
1/4 cup melted butter

FILLING

1/4 cup brown sugar, firmly packed
2 tbs. wheat germ
1/4 cup chopped pecans **or** walnuts
1/2 tsp. cinnamon

Preheat oven to 450°F. Stir together Quick Mix, baking soda and raisins. Mix together sour cream and milk. Stir into dry ingredients. Knead gently twelve times. Roll dough to a 1/4-inch thick rectangle of about 10 x 12 inches. Brush with melted butter. Combine filling ingredients. Sprinkle filling over dough. Roll as for jelly roll (starting at long end). Seal ends. Cut into 1-inch slices. Place cut side down on ungreased baking sheet. Bake for 12 minutes, or until golden brown. Makes 12 pinwheels.

HANNAH'S RIESKA BREAD

Serve this traditional flat Finnish bread hot from the oven with butter.

1-1/2 cups unbleached all-purpose flour
3/4 cup barley flour
1-1/2 tsp. baking powder
1/2 tsp. **each** baking soda and salt
2 tbs. sugar
1/4 cup butter **or** margarine
1 cup buttermilk

Preheat oven to 425°F. Stir together all-purpose flour, barley flour, baking powder, baking soda, salt and sugar. Cut butter into dry ingredients until mixture resembles coarse cornmeal. Stir in buttermilk until a soft dough is formed. Roll or pat dough on a greased cookie sheet to make a 10-inch circle. Bake for 20 minutes, or until golden brown. Cut with a serrated knife. Makes 1 round loaf.

IRISH OATMEAL SODA BREAD

1-1/2 cups all-purpose flour
1/2 cup quick cooking oats
2-1/2 tsp. baking powder
1/2 tsp. baking soda
1/2 tsp. salt

2 tsp. caraway seeds
1 tbs. sugar
1/3 cup butter **or** margarine
1/2 cup currants **or** raisins
3/4 cup buttermilk

Preheat oven to 375°F. Stir together flour, oats, baking powder, baking soda, salt, caraway seeds and sugar. Cut butter into dry ingredients until the mixture resembles coarse cornmeal. Stir in currants. Add buttermilk and stir until blended. Knead gently twelve times. Shape dough into a 7-inch circle on an ungreased baking sheet. Cut large "X" 1/4-inch deep across the top of entire dough. Bake for 30 minutes, or until golden brown. Cut in wedges to serve. Makes 1 loaf.

Wholesome Coffee Cakes

Wake up your "sleepy heads" with the heavenly aroma of coffee cake baking in the oven. It's possible, even on busy mornings, by using our Quick Mix Coffee Cake recipe. And, there are five different toppings to choose from.

Make early morning minutes count by doing most of the preliminary preparation the night before: Measure the Quick Mix or dry ingredients in a mixing bowl. Combine the milk, eggs and honey (liquid ingredients) and refrigerate. Mix the topping ingredients and set aside. All you have to do in the morning is preheat the oven, mix the batter and sprinkle on the topping. Less than five minutes will do it!

The same pre-preparation steps will work for many of the quick bread recipes in this book. It is an especially handy technique when preparing for guests.

Here are a few hints for making perfect coffee cakes every time:

• If the recipe calls for butter or margarine, allow it to soften at room temperature. Then, beat it until it becomes creamy.

• When adding dry ingredients to a creamed mixture alternately with the liquid ingredients, be sure not to overmix.

• Coffee cake is done when a toothpick inserted into the middle comes out clean. It will also start to pull away from the sides of the pan. Don't overbake.

QUICK MIX COFFEE CAKE

For those hectic mornings when you still want something good to eat, try this speedy recipe. Choose a topping from pages 128 and 129.

1/2 cup milk
1 egg
1/3 cup honey **or** sugar
2 cups Quick Mix (All-Purpose **or** Buttermilk, see pages 18 and 19)

Preheat oven to 400°F. Combine milk, egg and honey. Add them to Quick Mix. Stir until just blended. Pour batter into a greased and floured baking pan (8 x 8 x 2 inches). Spread with desired topping and bake for 20 minutes, or until done. Makes 1 coffee cake.

QUICK CHANGE COFFEE CAKE

Surprise! Five different coffee cakes can be made from this basic recipe! Simply choose your favorite topping from the list on pages 128 and 129.

1/2 cup **each** butter **or** margarine (softened) and honey **or** sugar
1 egg
2 cups all-purpose flour
1 tbs. baking powder
1/2 tsp. salt
1 tbs. grated lemon **or** orange peel (optional)
2/3 cup milk when using honey (3/4 cup milk when using sugar)
1/2 tsp. vanilla

Preheat oven to 400°F. Cream butter and honey. Mix in egg. Stir together flour, baking powder, salt and lemon peel. Add dry ingredients to creamed mixture alternately with the milk and vanilla. Pour batter into a greased and floured baking pan (9 x 9 x 2 inches). Spread desired topping over batter. Bake for 25 to 30 minutes, or until cake tests done. Makes 1 coffee cake.

COFFEE CAKE TOPPINGS

Make each topping by first combining the dry ingredients. Then, cut the butter or margarine into the dry ingredients until the mixture is crumbly. Spread over the coffee cake batter and bake as directed in coffee cake recipes.

GRANOLA TOPPING

1 cup granola
1/3 cup brown sugar, firmly packed
1/2 tsp. cinnamon
3 tbs. butter **or** margarine, softened

COCONUT TOPPING

1 cup shredded coconut
1/2 cup chopped pecans **or** walnuts
1/3 cup brown sugar, firmly packed
1/4 cup butter **or** margarine, softened

PECAN WHEAT GERM TOPPING

1/2 cup chopped pecans
1/2 cup wheat germ
1/3 cup brown sugar, firmly packed
1/4 cup butter **or** margarine, softened

CINNAMON SUGAR TOPPING

3 tbs. flour (whole wheat **or** unbleached all-purpose)
1/3 cup brown sugar, firmly packed
1/2 cup chopped pecans **or** walnuts
1 tsp. cinnamon
1/4 cup butter **or** margarine, softened

APPLE CHEESE TOPPING

Arrange one cup peeled, thinly sliced apples on top of batter, then add this crumbled mixture:

1/2 cup quick cooking oats
1/2 cup shredded Cheddar cheese
1/3 cup brown sugar, firmly packed
1/4 cup butter **or** margarine, softened

APPLE GRAHAM COFFEE CAKE

Graham cracker crumbs give this coffee cake a different flavor. Bits of shredded apple and nuts make it perfect.

1/4 cup butter **or** margarine, softened
1/2 cup brown sugar, firmly packed
1 egg
1 cup graham cracker crumbs
1 cup unbleached all-purpose flour
2 tsp. baking powder
1/2 tsp. baking soda

1/4 tsp. salt
1/2 tsp. allspice
1 tsp. cinnamon
1/4 cup chopped almonds **or** walnuts
1 cup shredded, peeled apple
1/4 cup milk
powdered sugar (optional)

Preheat oven to 375°F. Cream butter and sugar. Mix in egg. Stir together graham cracker crumbs, flour, baking powder, baking soda, salt, allspice, cinnamon and nuts. Stir dry ingredients into creamed mixture alternately with apple and milk. Spread batter into a greased and floured baking pan (8 x 8 x 2 inches). Bake for 35 minutes, or until cake tests done. Cool and dust with powdered sugar. Makes 1 coffee cake.

AVOCADO ORANGE COFFEE CAKE

2 cups all-purpose flour
3/4 cup brown sugar, firmly packed
1 tbs. baking powder
1/2 tsp. salt
1 tsp. cinnamon
1/2 cup chopped pecans **or** walnuts
3/4 cup mashed avocado
1/4 cup oil
1 egg
3/4 cup orange juice

ORANGE GLAZE:

1/2 cup powdered sugar
1 tsp. grated orange peel
1 tbs. orange juice

Preheat oven to 400°F. Stir together flour, brown sugar, baking powder, salt, cinnamon and nuts. Mix avocado, oil, egg and orange juice together well. Add this mixture to dry ingredients. Stir until just blended. Spread batter into a greased and floured baking pan (9 x 9 x 2 inches). Bake for 30 minutes, or until cake tests done. Combine glaze ingredients. Spread glaze over warm cake. Makes 1 coffee cake.

BANANA WHEAT GERM COFFEE CAKE

1/2 cup butter **or** margarine, softened
2/3 cup honey
2 eggs
1-1/4 cups **each** whole wheat flour and wheat germ
2 tsp. baking powder
1 tsp. baking soda
1/2 tsp. salt
1 cup shredded coconut
1/2 cup buttermilk
1 cup mashed banana

Preheat oven to 350°F. Cream butter and honey. Mix in eggs. Stir together flour, wheat germ, baking powder, baking soda, salt and coconut. Add dry ingredients to creamed mixture alternately with buttermilk and banana. Pour batter into a greased and floured tube or bundt pan (10 inch). Bake for 1 hour, or until cake tests done. Cool in pan for 10 minutes, then turn out on wire rack. Sprinkle with powdered sugar. Makes 1 coffee cake.

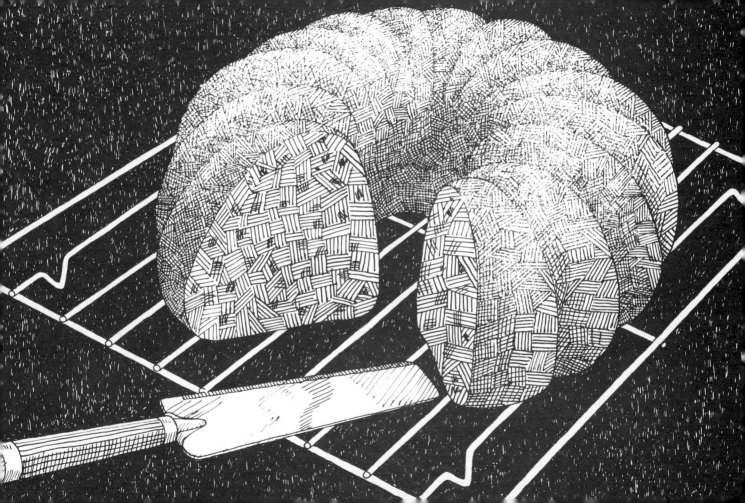

FABULOUS COFFEE CAKE

This is an unusual, absolutely delicious coffee cake.

1 cup butter **or** margarine, softened
1-1/2 cups brown sugar, firmly packed
2 eggs
3 cups all-purpose flour
2 tsp. baking soda
1/2 tsp. salt
1 tsp. cinnamon
1/2 tsp. **each** allspice and cloves

1 cup chopped walnuts
2 cups chopped dates
12 oz. can beer

LEMON GLAZE:
1 cup powdered sugar
2 tbs. lemon juice
1 tsp. grated lemon peel

Preheat oven to 350°F. Cream butter and sugar. Mix in eggs. Stir together flour, baking soda, salt, cinnamon, allspice, cloves, walnuts and dates. Add the dry ingredients to the creamed mixture alternately with beer. Pour batter into a greased and floured tube pan (10 inches). Bake for 1 hour and 15 minutes, or until cake tests done. Cool in pan for about 10 minutes, then turn out on wire rack. Spread on Lemon Glaze. Makes 1 coffee cake.

PINEAPPLE CARROT COFFEE CAKE

1-1/2 cups all-purpose flour
3/4 cup brown sugar, firmly packed
2-1/2 tsp. baking powder
1/2 tsp. salt
1 tsp. cinnamon
1 cup shredded carrots
1/2 cup chopped nuts
1/4 cup oil
1 egg

8 oz. can crushed pineapple, undrained
1 tsp. vanilla

CREAM CHEESE TOPPING:
3 oz. cream cheese
3 tbs. powdered sugar
1 tbs. milk
1/2 tsp. vanilla

Preheat oven to 350°F. Stir together flour, brown sugar, baking powder, salt, cinnamon, carrots and nuts. Mix the oil, egg, pineapple and vanilla together well. Add this mixture to the dry ingredients. Stir until just blended. Pour batter into a greased and floured baking pan (9 x 9 x 2 inches). Bake for 40 minutes, or until cake tests done. Cool, combine topping ingredients until creamy. Spread on coffee cake. Makes 1 coffee cake.

OATMEAL COCONUT COFFEE CAKE

A lunchbox treat for children.

1 cup quick-cooking oats
1/2 cup butter **or** margarine, cut into 5 slices
1-1/3 cups boiling water
3/4 cup sugar
3/4 cup brown sugar, firmly packed
2 eggs
3/4 cup whole wheat flour
3/4 cup unbleached all-purpose flour } **or** 1-1/2 cups all-purpose flour
2 tsp. baking powder
1 tsp. baking soda
1/4 tsp. salt
1 tsp. cinnamon
1/2 tsp. nutmeg
Coconut Topping (see page 137)

Preheat oven to 350°F. Combine oats, butter and boiling water. Let stand for 20 minutes. Beat together sugars and eggs. Stir together flour, baking powder, baking soda, salt, cinnamon and nutmeg. Add dry ingredients to sugar and eggs alternately with oats mixture. Pour batter into a greased and floured baking pan (9 x 13 inches). Bake for 35 minutes, or until cake tests done. Spread with topping and broil until the topping is golden brown. Serve warm. Makes 1 coffee cake.

COCONUT TOPPING:

1/3 cup butter **or** margarine, melted
3/4 cup brown sugar, firmly packed
1/4 cup milk
1 cup coconut
1 cup chopped nuts

Combine ingredients. Use as directed.

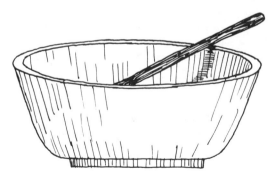

CHUCK'S CHOCOLATE CHIP COFFEE CAKE

1/2 cup butter **or** margarine, softened
3/4 cup sugar
2 eggs
2 cups unbleached all-purpose flour
1 tbs. baking powder
1/2 tsp. salt
1 cup milk
1 tsp. vanilla
1 cup mini chocolate chips

TOPPING:

1/2 cup chopped pecans **or** walnuts
1 tbs. sugar

Preheat oven to 350°F. Cream butter and sugar. Mix in eggs. Stir together flour, baking powder and salt. Add dry ingredients to creamed mixture alternately with milk and vanilla. Stir in chocolate chips. Spread batter into a greased and floured baking pan (9 x 9 x 2 inches). Combine topping ingredients. Sprinkle on topping and bake for 40 minutes, or until cake tests done. Makes 1 coffee cake.

BERTHA'S COFFEE CAKE

1-1/2 cups unbleached all-purpose flour
1/2 cup brown sugar, firmly packed
1/3 cup sugar
1 tsp. cinnamon
1/2 tsp. **each** nutmeg and ginger
1/2 cup oil

Preheat oven to 350°F. Stir together flour, sugars and spices. Blend in oil. **Set aside 1/2 cup of this mixture.** To the remainder add:

2 tsp. baking powder   1 egg
1/2 tsp. baking soda   1/2 cup sour cream
1/2 tsp. salt

Mix well and spread in a greased and floured baking pan (8 x 8 x 2 inches). Sprinkle the reserved mixture over the batter. Bake for 30 minutes, or until cake tests done. Makes 1 coffee cake.

PRUNE COFFEE CAKE

1/2 cup butter **or** margarine, softened
1-1/2 cups sugar
3 eggs
2 tsp. vanilla
2-1/2 cups all-purpose flour
2 tsp. baking powder
1 tsp. baking soda
1/2 tsp. salt

1 tsp. cinnamon
1 tsp. allspice
1/2 tsp. cloves
1 cup buttermilk
1 cup chopped pecans **or** walnuts
1 cup chopped dried prunes
powdered sugar (optional)

Preheat oven to 350°F. Cream butter and sugar. Mix in eggs and vanilla. Stir together flour, baking powder, baking soda, salt, cinnamon, allspice and cloves. Add dry ingredients to creamed mixture alternately with buttermilk. Stir in nuts and prunes. Pour batter into a greased and floured tube or bundt pan (10 inches). Bake for 65 minutes or until cake tests done. Cool in pan for 5 minutes, then turn out on wire rack. Dust with powdered sugar. Makes 1 coffee cake.

SPICY PUMPKIN COFFEE CAKE

2 cups Quick Mix (All-Purpose **or** Buttermilk, pages 18 and 19)
1/2 cup brown sugar, firmly packed
1/2 tsp. cinnamon
1/4 tsp. **each** ginger and cloves
1/2 cup raisins
1/2 cup chopped nuts
1/4 cup milk
2 eggs
3/4 cup canned pumpkin

TOPPING:

2 tbs. Quick Mix
1/4 cup brown sugar, firmly packed
1/2 tsp. cinnamon
2 tbs. chopped pecans **or** walnuts
2 tbs. butter **or** margarine

Preheat oven to 350°F. Stir together Quick Mix, brown sugar, cinnamon, ginger, cloves, raisins and nuts. Mix milk, eggs and pumpkin together well. Add liquid ingredients to dry ingredients. Stir until just blended. Spread batter in greased and floured baking pan (8 x 8 x 2 inches). Prepare topping: Combine dry ingredients. Cut in butter until mixture is crumbly. Sprinkle topping over cake batter. Bake for 40 minutes, or until cake tests done. Serve warm. Makes 1 coffee cake.

STREUSEL COFFEE CAKE

Streusel and apple slices swirl through this rich coffee cake.

1 cup butter or margarine
1-1/2 cups sugar
2 eggs
1-1/2 cups whole wheat flour
1-1/2 cups unbleached all-purpose flour
1 tbs. baking powder

1/2 tsp. salt
1 cup milk
1/2 cup brown sugar
3/4 cup chopped walnuts **or** pecans
1 tbs. cinnamon
1 apple, thinly sliced

Preheat oven to 350°F. Cream butter and sugar. Mix in eggs. Stir together dry ingredients. Add to creamed mixture alternately with milk. In a small bowl combine brown sugar, nuts and cinnamon. Grease and flour a 10-inch tube pan. Spread the ingredients as follows: 1/3 batter, 1/3 streusel, 1/2 apple slices; 1/3 batter, 1/3 streusel, 1/2 apple slices; 1/3 batter and top with remaining streusel. Bake 1 hour and 10 minutes or until done. Serve warm.

UPSIDE DOWN COFFEE CAKE

Don't limit yourself to just pineapple for this upside down treat. Try apples or bananas instead! See page 145 for the variations.

1/2 cup butter **or** margarine, softened
1/2 cup sugar
1 egg
1 cup whole wheat flour
1 cup unbleached all-purpose flour } **or** 2 cups all-purpose flour
1 tbs. baking powder
1/2 tsp. salt
2/3 cup milk
3 tbs. butter **or** margarine
1/4 cup brown sugar, firmly packed
"Topping" variation (see page 145)

Preheat oven to 375°F. Cream butter and sugar. Mix in egg. Stir together flour, baking powder and salt. Add dry ingredients to creamed mixture alternately with milk. Set aside. Melt 3 tablespoons of butter in a baking pan (9 x 9 x 2 inches) in oven. Sprinkle brown sugar over butter. Arrange fruit, cut side up, in an attractive pattern in the pan, **or** sprinkle on coconut and pecans. Spread batter in pan and bake for 30 to 35 minutes. Remove from oven and immediately invert pan, but keep pan over the cake for several minutes. Remove pan and serve warm. Makes 1 coffee cake.

"TOPPING" VARIATIONS FOR UPSIDE DOWN COFFEE CAKE

- 9 pineapple rings with a maraschino cherry in the center of each.
- 2 cups peeled apple slices, 1/4 cup raisins, 1/4 cup walnut halves and 1/2 teaspoon of cinnamon
- 1 cup banana slices. Brush the cake with 3 tablespoons rum before serving.
- 1 cup fruit cocktail or sliced canned fruit, drained well. Brush the cake with 3 tablespoons brandy before serving.
- 1/2 cup coconut and 1/2 cup pecans.

BLUEBERRY BUCKLE COFFEE CAKE

Great-grandma used fresh blueberries for her buckle. If they are not in season use canned or frozen ones, but be sure to rinse and drain well.

1/2 cup butter **or** margarine, softened
1/2 cup sugar
1 egg
1 cup whole wheat flour
1 cup unbleached all-purpose flour } **or** 2 cups all-purpose flour
2-1/2 tsp. baking powder
1/2 tsp. baking soda
1/2 tsp. salt
2/3 cup buttermilk
2 cups blueberries
Topping (see page 147)

Preheat oven to 375°F. Cream butter and sugar. Mix in egg. Stir together flour, baking powder, baking soda and salt. Add the dry ingredients to creamed mixture alternately with buttermilk. Gently, stir in blueberries. Spread batter in a greased and floured baking pan (9 x 9 x 2 inches). Sprinkle with topping. Bake for 50 minutes, or until cake tests done. Serve warm. Makes 1 coffee cake.

TOPPING

1/2 cup sugar
1/3 cup flour (whole wheat **or** all-purpose)
1/2 tsp. cinnamon
1/4 cup butter **or** margarine, softened

Combine sugar, flour and cinnamon. Cut butter into dry ingredients until mixture is crumbly. Use as directed.

SUPER NUTRITIOUS COFFEE CAKE

1/2 cup soy flour
1 cup all-purpose flour
1/3 cup wheat germ
2 tbs. unprocessed bran
1/3 cup instant nonfat dry milk
1 tbs. baking powder
1 tsp. baking soda
1/4 tsp. salt
1/2 cup **each** chopped dates **or** raisins and chopped nuts
1 cup yogurt
1 egg
1/4 cup oil
1 tbs. molasses
3 tbs. honey
2 tbs. orange juice
Topping (see page 149)

Preheat oven to 350°F. Stir together flours, wheat germ, bran, instant milk, baking powder, baking soda, salt, dates and nuts. Mix yogurt, egg, oil, molasses, honey and orange juice together well. Add this mixture to dry ingredients. Stir until just blended. Pour batter into a greased and floured baking pan (9 x 9 x 2 inches). Sprinkle on topping. Bake for 35 minutes, or until cake tests done. Makes 1 coffee cake.

TOPPING

1/4 cup wheat germ
1/3 cup date sugar, **or** brown sugar, firmly packed
1/4 cup chopped pecans **or** walnuts
1 tsp. cinnamon
1/4 cup butter **or** margarine, softened

Stir together wheat germ, date sugar, nuts and cinnamon. Cut butter into the dry ingredients until mixture is crumbly. Use as directed.

GINGERBREAD

Simply heavenly served warm with its own special buttermilk glaze.

1/2 cup butter **or** margarine
1/2 cup dark molasses
1/4 cup honey **or** sugar
1 egg
1 cup whole wheat flour
1 cup unbleached all-purpose flour } **or** 2 cups all-purpose flour
2 tsp. baking powder
1-1/2 tsp. baking soda
1/2 tsp. salt
1 tsp. **each** ground ginger and cinnamon
1/4 tsp. **each** nutmeg and ground cloves
1/2 cup buttermilk

Preheat oven to 350°F. Cream butter. Mix in molasses, honey egg and vanilla.

Combine dry ingredients. Stir into butter mixture alternately with buttermilk. Pour batter into a greased and floured baking pan (9 x 9 x 2 inches). Bake 40 minutes or until done. Serve warm with Buttermilk Glaze.

BUTTERMILK GLAZE

3 tbs. butter **or** margarine
3 tbs. honey **or** sugar
1/4 cup buttermilk
1/4 tsp. baking soda
1/2 tsp. vanilla

Combine ingredients in a small saucepan. Cook over low heat until syrupy, about 15 minutes, stirring frequently. Spoon over hot gingerbread and serve.

Perfect Pancakes, Popovers and Wonderful Waffles

Who can resist the wonderful aroma of fresh baked pancakes, popovers or waffles in the morning? Serve your breakfast favorites with homemade "maple" syrup, honey butter or spicy applesauce (see pages 178, 179 and 182). For a quick dinner sure to please, serve sherried crab sauce over pancakes or waffles (see page 184).

Follow these suggestions for the best pancakes, popovers and waffles:

● For pancakes and waffles, stir together the liquid and dry ingredients only until they are just moistened. Do not overmix. The batter will be slightly lumpy.

● For lighter pancakes or waffles, separate the egg and beat the white until stiff, but not dry. Fold beaten white into batter.

● Cook pancakes at 380°F., unless otherwise directed.

● It is only necessary to lightly oil the surface of the pan for the first batch of pancakes.

● Pancakes are cooked most easily and with the best results on an electric griddle or in an electric frying pan.

- Pancakes are done when bubbles appear, and the edges of the "cake" are dry. Also check the underside of the pancake to see if it is well browned. Merely pick up an edge of the "cake" with a spatula and take a peek. Remember, the second side of the pancake takes less time to cook. Serve immediately.
- For waffles, preheat the waffle iron to the hottest temperature possible. When a drop of water sizzles on the surface, add the batter.
- Spoon or pour the waffle batter onto the preheated iron to about one inch from the edge. This will allow the waffle to expand and rise without spilling over the edges of the iron.
- Waffles are done when they have stopped steaming, or when they have reached the desired degree of brownness. The longer you bake waffles, the crisper they will be.
- For popovers beat ingredients together until smooth.
- Perfect popovers are high, light and have a crisp, golden brown shell.
- Do not open the oven while popovers are baking — they will collapse!
- Prick popovers with a fork or skewer as soon as you remove from the oven, to release steam. Serve immediately.

QUICK STACK

Rushing in the morning? Make Quick Mix Pancakes!

2 cups Quick Mix (All-Purpose **or** Buttermilk, pages 18 and 19)
1 tbs. sugar **or** honey
1 egg
1-1/4 cups milk

Stir together Quick Mix and sugar. Mix egg and milk together well. Add this mixture to dry ingredients. Stir only until moistened. If thinner pancakes are desired, add more milk. Pour or spoon batter onto a hot griddle or frying pan. Cook on both sides until golden brown. Makes about 8 medium-sized pancakes. Serve hot with butter, syrup, honey or jam.

MELT-IN-YOUR-MOUTH PANCAKES

Watch your family's eyes light up when these are served!

3/4 cup whole wheat flour
3/4 cup unbleached all-purpose flour } **or** 1-1/2 cups all-purpose flour
2-1/2 tsp. baking powder
1/2 tsp. salt
1 tbs. sugar **or** honey
1 egg
1-1/4 cups milk
3 tbs. melted butter, margarine **or** oil

Stir together flour, baking powder, salt and sugar. Mix egg, milk and butter together well. Add this mixture to dry ingredients. Stir only until moistened. If thinner pancakes are desired, add more milk. Pour or spoon batter onto a hot griddle or frying pan. Cook on both sides until golden brown. Makes about 10 medium-sized pancakes. Serve hot with butter, syrup, honey or jam.

PANCAKE VARIATIONS

Add any one of the following ingredients to a basic pancake batter.

- 1/2 cup chopped dates
- 3/4 cup blueberries, rinsed and drained if canned or drozen
- 1/3 cup fried bacon, crumbled
- 1/2 cup chopped pecans **or** walnuts
- Replace milk with buttermilk and add 1/2 tsp. baking soda.
- Substitute 1/2 cup quick-cooking oats for 1/2 cup flour
- **Grandpa Jack's Peach Pancakes** Replace 1/4 cup milk with 1/4 cup canned peach juice and add 1/2 cup chopped canned peaches.
- Spoon 2 tablespoons fresh fruit on a pancake, roll it up and dust with powdered sugar.

BOB'S BUTTERMILK PANCAKES

Add blueberries to this recipe and come up with everybody's favorite — blueberry pancakes!

2 cups all-purpose flour
1 tsp. baking soda
1/2 tsp. salt
2 cups buttermilk
3 eggs, separated
1/4 cup melted butter **or** margarine
1 cup blueberries (optional, rinsed and drained if canned or frozen)

Stir together flour, baking soda and salt. Combine buttermilk, egg yolks and melted butter. Add this mixture to dry ingredients. Stir until just moistened. Beat egg whites until stiff. Fold into batter. Gently fold in blueberries, if desired. Pour or spoon batter onto a hot griddle or frying pan. Cook on both sides until golden brown. Makes about 18 medium-sized pancakes.

AL'S BUCKWHEAT PANCAKES

These old-time favorites have a flavor all their own.

1-1/2 cups whole wheat flour
1/2 cup buckwheat flour
1 tbs. baking powder
1/2 tsp. salt
2 cups milk
1/2 cup oil
2 tbs. molasses (optional)
3 eggs, separated

Stir together wheat flour, buckwheat flour, baking powder and salt. Mix milk, oil, molasses and egg yolks together well. Add this mixture to dry ingredients. Stir only until moistened. Beat egg whites until stiff. Fold into batter. Pour or spoon batter onto a hot griddle or frying pan. Cook on both sides until golden brown. Makes about 16 medium-sized pancakes.

SOUR CREAM PANCAKES

1 cup whole wheat flour
1/2 cup wheat germ
2 tbs. unprocessed bran
1-1/2 tsp. baking powder
1/4 tsp. baking soda
1/2 tsp. salt
1/2 cup sour cream
1 egg, separated
2 tbs. honey **or** molasses
1-1/4 cups milk
3 tbs. melted butter, margarine **or** oil

Stir together flour, wheat germ, bran, baking powder, baking soda and salt. Mix sour cream, egg yolk, honey, milk and butter together well. Add this mixture to the dry ingredients. Stir until just moistened. Beat egg white until stiff. Fold into batter. Pour or spoon batter onto a hot griddle or frying pan. Cook on both sides until golden brown. Makes 10 to 12 medium-sized pancakes.

NUTRITION-PACKED PANCAKES

When the kids clamor for pancakes and you are thinking "nutrition," this hot-cake is the perfect solution.

1/2 cup soy flour
1/2 cup whole wheat flour   } **or** 1 cup all-purpose flour
1/2 cup unbleached all-purpose flour
2 tbs. **each** wheat germ, unprocessed bran and instant nonfat dry milk
1 tbs. baking powder
1/2 tsp. baking soda
1/4 tsp. salt
2 tsp. grated orange peel
1/2 cup yogurt
2 eggs, separated
3 tbs. oil
1 tbs. molasses **or** honey
1 cup orange juice

Stir together flours, wheat germ, bran, instant milk, baking powder, baking soda, salt and orange peel. Mix yogurt, egg yolks, oil, molasses and orange juice together well. Add this mixture to the dry ingredients. Stir until just moistened. Beat egg whites until stiff. Fold into batter. Pour or spoon batter onto a moderately hot (350°F.) griddle or frying pan. (Soy flour browns quickly.) Cook on both sides until golden brown. Makes 10 to 12 pancakes.

CREPES

The popularity of crepes has grown tremendously over the last few years. Serve these delicious thin "pancakes" for breakfast, lunch, dinner or dessert.

1/2 cup milk
1/2 cup water
2 eggs
1 cup unbleached all-purpose flour
1/2 tsp. salt
oil (a few drops for each crepe)

Combine all ingredients in blender container. Blend until smooth. Refrigerate batter for two hours or overnight. Heat crepe pan or small frying pan to a fairly high temperature. Brush pan with oil. Pour about 2 tablespoons of batter into pan. Tilt quickly to coat pan with batter. Pour off excess batter. When browned on the bottom, turn. Cook until brown. Repeat process using the remaining batter. Grease pan between crepes. Makes about 14 crepes. To serve, fill each crepe with a dinner or dessert filling or sauce (see pages 181 through 185).

For dessert crepes, add the following ingredients to the basic crepe batter.

1 tbs. brandy
1/2 tsp. grated orange **or** lemon peel
1 tbs. sugar

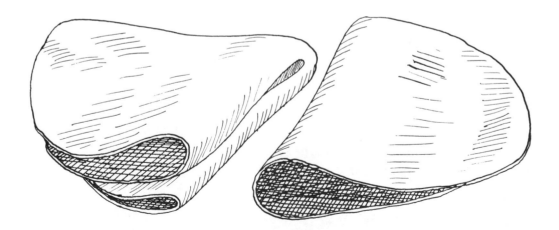

POPOVERS

Perfect popovers are high and light with a golden brown shell.

1 cup milk
2 eggs
1 tbs. melted butter **or** margarine **or** oil

1 cup unbleached all-purpose flour
1/4 tsp. salt

Preheat oven to 375°F. Combine all ingredients and mix until smooth. Pour batter into well-greased custard cups or muffin pans 1/2 full. Bake 45 to 50 minutes. Do not open oven or popovers may collapse. Prick with fork or skewer to let steam escape. Serve immediately. Makes 6 large or 12 small popovers.

VARIATIONS

Whole wheat — replace 1/2 cup all-purpose flour with 1/2 cup whole wheat flour.
Parmesan — sprinkle batter with Parmesan cheese before baking.
Cheese — add 1/4 cup shredded cheese to batter.

QUICK MIX WAFFLES

Be creative with the numerous waffle variations on page 170.

2 cups Quick Mix (All-Purpose **or** Buttermilk, pages 18 and 19)
2 tbs. honey **or** sugar
2 eggs, separated
1 cup milk

Measure Quick Mix into bowl. Mix honey, egg yolks and milk together well. Add this mixture to dry ingredients. Stir until just blended. Beat egg whites until stiff. Fold into batter. Pour or spoon batter onto a hot waffle iron. Cook waffles to desired doneness. Makes 4 to 6 waffles.

CRISPY WAFFLES

When you are baking waffles, double the recipe and freeze the leftovers. Just pop them into the toaster when you have the urge for a waffle, but not the time to mix up a fresh batch.

1 cup whole wheat flour
1 cup unbleached all-purpose flour } **or** 2 cups all-purpose flour
1 tbs. baking powder
1/2 tsp. salt
2 tbs. sugar
2 eggs, separated
6 tbs. melted butter, margarine **or** oil
1-1/2 cups milk

Stir together flour, baking powder, salt and sugar. Mix egg yolks, butter and milk together well. Add this mixture to dry ingredients. Stir until just blended. Beat egg whites until stiff. Fold into batter. Pour or spoon batter onto a hot waffle iron. Cook waffles to desired doneness. Makes 5 to 7 waffles.

WAFFLE VARIATIONS

Add any one of the following ingredients to basic waffle batter.

- 2/3 cup diced banana and 1/4 cup unprocessed bran
- 1/2 cup grated apple and 1/2 teaspoon cinnamon
- 1/2 cup chopped dates and 1/4 cup chopped nuts
- 3/4 cup blueberries (rinsed and drained if they are canned or frozen)
- 1/3 cup coconut and 1/3 cup chopped nuts
- 1/2 cup chopped pecans **or** walnuts
- 1/3 cup shredded cheddar cheese and 1/4 cup crisp bacon, crumbled
- Replace the milk with buttermilk and add 1/2 teaspoon baking soda.
- Reduce the butter, margarine or oil to 1/4 cup and add 1/3 cup chunky peanut butter to the liquid ingredients.
- Replace 3/4 cup milk with 3/4 cup orange juice and add 1 tablespoon grated orange peel.

CORN WAFFLES

Top with chili (see page 185) for a great meal-in-a-hurry.

1-1/2 cups all-purpose flour
1/2 cup yellow cornmeal
1 tbs. baking powder
1/2 tsp. salt
2 tbs. sugar
1 cup canned whole kernal corn, drained
2 eggs, separated
6 tbs. melted butter, margarine **or** oil
1-1/2 cups milk

Stir together flour, cornmeal, baking powder, salt and sugar. Mix corn, egg yolks, butter and milk together well. Add this mixture to dry ingredients. Stir until just blended. Beat egg whites until stiff. Fold into batter. Pour or spoon batter onto a hot waffle iron. Cook waffles to desired doneness. Makes 5 to 7 waffles.

GINGERBREAD WAFFLES

Serve these waffles with warm spicy applesauce (see page 182).

2 cups all-purpose flour
1 tbs. baking powder
1/2 tsp. salt
1/2 tsp. cinnamon
1/4 tsp. **each** ginger and nutmeg

2 tbs. sugar
1/2 cup molasses
2 eggs, separated
6 tbs. melted butter, margarine **or** oil
1 cup milk

Stir together flour, baking powder, salt, cinnamon, ginger, nutmeg and sugar. Mix molasses, egg yolks, butter and milk together well. Add this mixture to dry ingredients. Stir until just blended. Beat egg whites until stiff. Fold into batter. Pour or spoon batter onto a hot waffle iron. Cook waffles to desired doneness. Makes 5 to 7 waffles.

SOUR CREAM WALNUT WAFFLES

1 cup whole wheat flour
1 cup unbleached all-purpose flour } **or** 2 cups all-purpose flour
2-1/2 tsp. baking powder
1/2 tsp. **each** baking soda and salt
2/3 cup chopped walnuts
2 tbs. sugar
2 eggs, separated
6 tbs. melted butter, margarine **or** oil
1-1/2 cups milk
3/4 cups sour cream

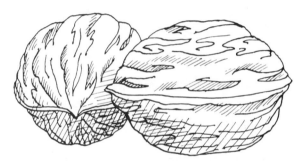

Stir together flour, baking powder, baking soda, salt, nuts and sugar. Mix egg yolks, butter, milk and sour cream together well. Add this mixture to dry ingredients. Stir until just blended. Beat egg whites until stiff. Fold into batter. Pour or spoon batter onto a hot waffle iron. Cook waffles to desired doneness. Makes 6 to 8 waffles.

CHRISTINE'S DANISH AEBLESKIVERS

Katherine's great grandmother brought this recipe and her aebleskiver pan to California from Denmark in the 1890's. The pan was handed down from mother to daughter for generations. Katherine is still using it! An aebleskiver pan is about 8 inches in diameter. It is basically a skillet with 7 indentations in which the aebleskiver batter cooks.

3/4 cup whole wheat flour
3/4 cup unbleached all-purpose flour } **or** 1-1/2 cups all-purpose flour
2 tsp. baking powder
1/2 tsp. salt
1 tbs. sugar
2 eggs, separated
1 cup milk
oil
aebleskiver pan
2 bananas **or** 1 small can of peaches, well drained (optional)
powdered sugar

Stir together flour, baking powder, salt, and sugar. Mix egg yolks and milk together well. Add this mixture to dry ingredients. Stir until just blended. Beat egg whites until stiff. Fold into batter. Heat aebleskiver pan. Spoon 1/2 teaspoon oil into each section and fill 2/3 full with batter. Cook over medium heat until bubbles appear. Turn aebleskivers with a fork or skewer and cook the other side until lightly browned. To vary flavor, add a slice of banana or peach to each before it is turned. Dust with powdered sugar and serve with butter and jam or syrup. Makes about 28 aebleskivers.

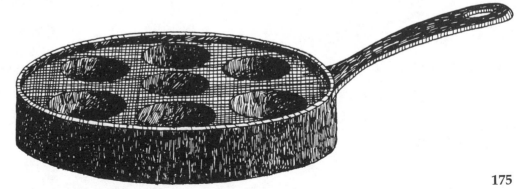

Versatile Syrups, Spreads and Sauces

You can be even more creative with our quick breads by "mixing and matching" with the syrups, spreads, flavored butters and sauces in this section. Turn biscuits, waffles or crepes into exciting and out-of-the ordinary dinner treats by serving with one of the following sauces. How do sherried crab waffles, crepes ratatouilles or cornbread squares topped with chili and garnished with grated cheese, sound for a quick and easy meal?

Make your own warm "maple" syrup and really do your favorite pancakes and waffles justice. And, the next time you bake a loaf of bread for a gift, include a little pot of one of the sweet or savory spreads. It will make your gift doubly delicious.

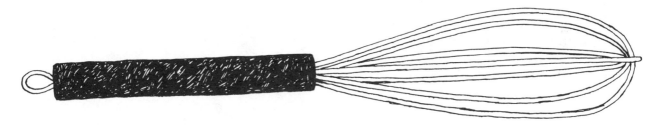

HOMEMADE "MAPLE" SYRUP

1 cup brown sugar, firmly packed
2/3 cup water

2 tbs. butter **or** margarine
1/2 tsp. maple **or** vanilla flavoring

Boil brown sugar and water in a saucepan for 5 minutes. Stir in butter or margarine and flavoring. Serve warm.

VARIATIONS FOR "MAPLE" SYRUP

Add any one of the following ingredients to one cup homemade "maple" syrup or commercial maple syrup. Heat in a saucepan and serve warm.

- 2 tsp. grated orange peel
- 1/4 cup chopped pecans and 2 tbs. butter **or** margarine
- 1/4 cup light cream
- 2 tbs. sherry, 2 tbs. butter **or** margarine, and dash of cinnamon and nutmeg

HONEY BUTTER SYRUP

Instead of pouring cold honey on your pancakes or waffles, why not try this warm syrup.

1 cup honey
1/4 cup butter

Heat in saucepan on medium heat until the butter melts. Serve warm.

VARIATIONS

Add any one of the following ingredients to the Honey Butter Syrup.
- 1/4 tsp. cinnamon and 1/4 tsp. nutmeg
- 2 tsp. grated orange peel
- 1/4 cup shredded coconut and 1/4 cup light cream **or** milk.

SWEET AND SAVORY BUTTERS

To make your quick breads extra special, try a sweet or savory butter spread on top.

Add one of the following suggestions to 1/2 cup of soft butter. If desired, whip the butter in the mixer until fluffy.

- 1/4 cup honey **or** maple syrup
- 2 tsp. grated lemon **or** orange peel and 1 tbs. powdered sugar **or** honey
- 1 peach, peeled and chopped, 1 tsp. lemon juice, 2 tbs. brown sugar **or** honey, dash cinnamon

HARD SAUCE:
- 1-1/2 cups powdered sugar, 1/2 tsp. vanilla, and 2 tbs. brandy, bourbon **or** rum
- 1 tbs. snipped parsley, 1/4 tsp. oregano, 1/4 tsp. dill and 1 clove minced garlic
- 2 tbs. snipped chives **or** parsley
- 3 tbs. Parmesan cheese, 1/4 tsp. marjoram and 1/4 tsp. basil

SWEET CREAM CHEESE SPREADS

Add one of the following to 8 ounces of softened cream cheese:

- 2 tsp. grated orange peel and 2 tbs. honey **or** sugar
- 3 tbs. orange marmalade
- 1/4 cup chopped dates **or** raisins
- 1/4 cup chopped nuts
- 3 tbs. maple syrup

TROPICAL FRUIT SPREAD

1 tbs. honey **or** sugar
1/3 cup crushed pineapple, drained
1 tsp. grated orange peel

1/4 cup shredded coconut
8 oz. pkg. cream cheese, softened

Mix the ingredients until blended.

BRANDIED FRUIT SAUCE

Serve with shortcake, pancakes, crepes or waffles.

21 oz. can cherry **or** blueberry pie filling
1 tsp. grated lemon peel
3 tbs. brandy
2 tbs. butter **or** margarine

Heat the above ingredients in a small saucepan until warm.

SPICY APPLESAUCE

Serve warm over pancakes or waffles.

1 lb. can applesauce
1 tbs. butter **or** margarine

1/4 tsp. cinnamon
1/4 tsp. nutmeg

Heat the above ingredients in a small saucepan until warm.

RATATOUILLE

A bountiful harvest of vegetables to serve with herb biscuits or muffins.

2 tbs. oil
1 large white onion, sliced
1 clove garlic, crushed
1 small eggplant, peeled and cubed
3 medium zucchini, thickly sliced
1/4 lb. fresh mushrooms, halved
3 carrots, peeled and sliced
1 small green pepper, cut in strips
2 large tomatoes, skinned and chunked
2 tbs. snipped parsley
1 tsp. **each** salt and basil

Saute onion and garlic in oil until tender. Add remaining ingredients and simmer covered for about 30 minutes, or until vegetables are done. Makes 5 to 6 servings.

SHERRIED CRAB SAUCE

A San Francisco favorite! Great over waffles.

2 tbs. butter **or** margarine
2 tsp. flour (whole wheat **or** all-purpose)
1 cup light cream **or** milk
1 cup crab meat **or** 7-1/2 oz. can crab, drained and flaked
salt and pepper to taste
dash nutmeg
3 tbs. dry sherry

Melt butter in saucepan. Stir in flour. Gradually add cream. Stir until thickened. Add remaining ingredients and heat until warm. Makes 6 servings.

CHILI

For a South-of-the-Border treat, serve piping hot chili over cornbread (see page 62). Add a green salad and you have a quick and easy meal.

1 tbs. oil
1 cup chopped onion
1 clove garlic, crushed
1 lb. ground beef
16 oz. can tomatoes, undrained
4 oz. can chopped green chiles
1 tsp. salt

1 tbs. chili powder (or more to taste)
1 tsp. ground cumin
1 bay leaf
1/2 tsp. oregano
1 whole small red pepper
16 oz. can red kidney beans, drained

In frying pan, saute onion and garlic in oil until tender. Add ground beef and brown. Drain fat. Stir in tomatoes, chiles, salt, chili powder, cumin, bay leaf, oregano and red pepper. Simmer covered for about two hours, stirring occasionally. Add a little water if chili is too thick. Add beans and heat until warm. Remove bay leaf and red pepper before serving. Makes 4 to 6 servings.

INDEX

QUICK MIX RECIPES

METRIC CONVERSION CHART

Liquid or Dry Measuring Cup (based on an 8 ounce cup)

1/4 cup = 60 ml
1/3 cup = 80 ml
1/2 cup = 125 ml
3/4 cup = 190 ml
1 cup = 250 ml
2 cups = 500 ml

Liquid or Dry Measuring Cup (based on a 10 ounce cup)

1/4 cup = 80 ml
1/3 cup = 100 ml
1/2 cup = 150 ml
3/4 cup = 230 ml
1 cup = 300 ml
2 cups = 600 ml

Liquid or Dry Teaspoon and Tablespoon

1/4 tsp. = 1.5 ml
1/2 tsp. = 3 ml
1 tsp. = 5 ml
3 tsp. = 1 tbs. = 15 ml

Temperatures

°F		°C
200	=	100
250	=	120
275	=	140
300	=	150
325	=	160
350	=	180
375	=	190
400	=	200
425	=	220
450	=	230
475	=	240
500	=	260
550	=	280

Pan Sizes (1 inch = 25 mm)

8-inch pan (round or square) = 200 mm x 200 mm
9-inch pan (round or square) = 225 mm x 225 mm
9 x 5 x 3-inch loaf pan = 225 mm x 125 mm x 75 mm
1/4 inch thickness = 5 mm
1/8 inch thickness = 2.5 mm

Pressure Cooker

100 Kpa = 15 pounds per square inch
70 Kpa = 10 pounds per square inch
35 Kpa = 5 pounds per square inch

Mass

1 ounce = 30 g
4 ounces = 1/4 pound = 125 g
8 ounces = 1/2 pound = 250 g
16 ounces = 1 pound = 500 g
2 pounds = 1 kg

Key (America uses an 8 ounce cup - Britain uses a 10 ounce cup)

ml = milliliter
l = liter
g = gram
K = Kilo (one thousand)
mm = millimeter
m = milli (a thousandth)
°F = degrees Fahrenheit

°C = degrees Celsius
tsp. = teaspoon
tbs. = tablespoon
Kpa = (pounds pressure per square inch)
This configuration is used for pressure cookers only.

Metric equivalents are rounded to conform to existing metric measuring utensils.

SERVE CREATIVE, EASY, NUTRITIOUS MEALS WITH NITTY GRITTY® COOKBOOKS

Waffles
The Coffee Book
The Bread Machine Cookbook
The Bread Machine Cookbook II
The Bread Machine Cookbook III
The Bread Machine Cookbook IV
The Sandwich Maker Cookbook
The Juicer Book
Bread Baking (traditional), revised
The Kid's Cookbook, revised
The Kid's Microwave Cookbook
15-Minute Meals for 1 or 2
Recipes for the 9x13 Pan
Turkey, the Magic Ingredient
Chocolate Cherry Tortes and Other Lowfat Delights

Lowfat American Favorites
Lowfat International Cuisine
The Hunk Cookbook
Now That's Italian!
Fabulous Fiber Cookery
Low Salt, Low Sugar, Low Fat Desserts
What's for Breakfast?
Healthy Cooking on the Run
Healthy Snacks for Kids
Creative Soups & Salads
Quick & Easy Pasta Recipes, revised
Muffins, Nut Breads and More
The Barbecue Book
The Wok
New Ways with Your Wok

Quiche & Soufflé Cookbook
Easy Microwave Cooking
Cooking for 1 or 2
Meals in Minutes
New Ways to Enjoy Chicken
Favorite Seafood Recipes
No Salt, No Sugar, No Fat Cookbook
New International Fondue Cookbook
Extra-Special Crockery Pot Recipes
Favorite Cookie Recipes
Authentic Mexican Cooking
Fisherman's Wharf Cookbook
The Creative Lunch Box

Write or call for our free catalog.
Bristol Publishing Enterprises, Inc.
P.O. Box 1737, San Leandro, CA 94577
(800)346-4889; in California (510)895-4461